Editor
Tim Dowley
Designer
Peter Wyart
Photographer
Clifford Shirley
Copy Editor
Mig Holder

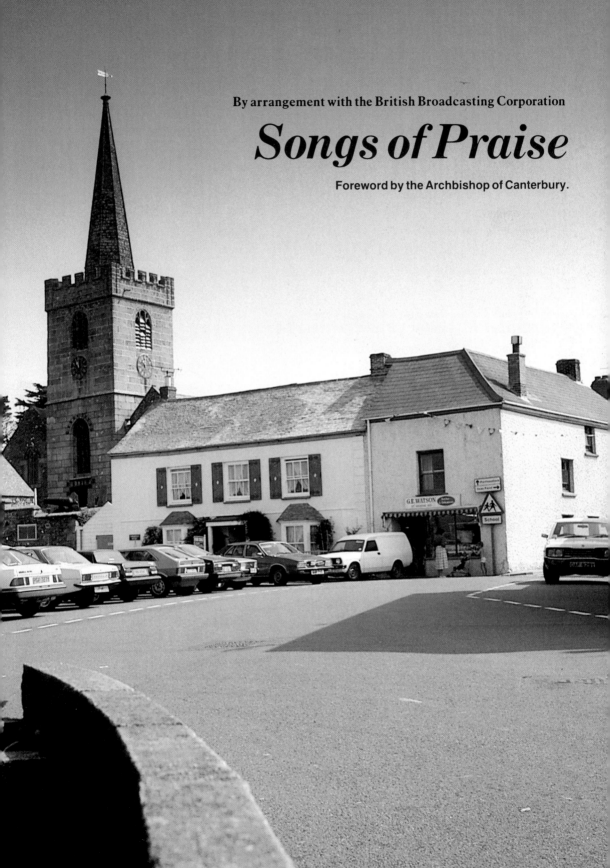

The centre of St Keverne, Cornwall.

By arrangement with the British Broadcasting Corporation

Songs of Praise

Foreword by the Archbishop of Canterbury.

Marshall Morgan & Scott

3 Beggarwood Lane,
Basingstoke,
Hants,
RG23 7LP, UK

Designed and produced for
Marshall Morgan & Scott
by Three's Company
12 Flitcroft St,
London WC2

Copyright © 1984
Marshall Morgan & Scott

First published by
Marshall Morgan & Scott

Hardback ISBN 0 551 01165 3

All the photographs in this
book have been specially
commissioned by Three's
Company from photographer
Clifford Shirley,
except the following:
BBC *27, 33, 34, 43, 50, 54, 61,
98, 101, 144*
Church of England *18, 19*
Tim Dowley *30/31, 31*
Wendy J. Dyer *102*
Jim Murray *47, 75, 99, 100,
103*
Liz Ryves-Brown *48, 76*
Peter Wyart *19, 54, 55, 88,
122*

Set in Century Schoolbook
by The Grange Press,
Southwick, Sussex

Printed in Great Britain by
Purnell & Sons Ltd,
Paulton, Bristol

Permissions
'Thine be the glory' copyright
World Student Christian
Federation. Used by permission.
'Be thou my Vision' from *The
Poem Book of the Gael*
selected and edited by
Eleanor Hull, published by
permission of the Editor's
Literary Estate and Chatto
& Windus.
'Lord of the Dance' by Sidney
Carter published by permission of Stainer & Bell Ltd.

Contents

Songs of Praise

This book consists of a number of interviews from Songs of Praise selected from many programmes broadcast during the last few years. They reflect some of the recurring themes, as well as the unending variety of the people, featured in Songs of Praise. The book also includes the words of many of the most popular hymns requested for the programme, and is illustrated with photographs of the interviewees, and of their homes, their towns and cities, their native countryside.

6

Foreword

by the Archbishop of Canterbury.

I regularly receive letters which mention the programme Songs of Praise, and so I have good reason to know what a popular and well-loved programme it is. It consistently earns a place in the ratings of the top hundred programmes. With audience figures of many millions, it is even more popular than programmes like Match of the Day, and it undoubtedly attracts many people who do not go to Church.

Some clergy complain that popular hymn-singing is a soft option for those who want religion without commitment: Songs of Praise has no sermon, no sacrament and no Creed. The audience is anonymous. Be that as it may, the programme touches a vein of spirituality which is deep in British experience.

Songs of Praise is usually set in a beautiful church building, often Anglican, but the congregation is gathered from all the local churches.

There is something liberating in watching Christians of all denominations and all ages joyfully and vigorously joining to sing the praises of God: and the short interviews with members of the congregation reveal a Christian hope often victorious over suffering and hardship.

The fact that Songs of Praise is very much an ecumenical venture greatly appeals to me. I hope this anthology, culled from the programme, will give pleasure and encouragement to many.
+ *Robert Cantuar*

From the producer . . .

Songs of Praise is a British institution. Every Sunday night from the height of summer to Easter Day millions of people in the British Isles stop what they are doing and turn on their tv sets to share in the Christian worship of a town or village, and to meet some of the Christian people who live there.

The exact number of viewers varies depending on the time of the year – in summer, for example, many are away on holiday or out for the day. By contrast in winter many older people, who cannot travel to their churches during the cold weather, stay at home and watch the programme.

However in recent years as many as nine million people have regularly watched the programme and, for special occasions, up to ten and a half million people have tuned in. What this means in practice is that this overtly religious programme has been one of the BBC's most popular programmes – sometimes even appearing in the Top Ten list for BBC-1 programmes, seldom out of the top fifty or sixty programmes on all channels in Britain, and never, even in summer, out of the top hundred.

Quite an achievement in professional television! A great deal of credit is due to the producers, directors, researchers and others who work virtually non-stop around the year to make not only Songs of Praise but also your Songs of Praise Choice series with Thora Hird and Home on Sunday, a sort of 'desert island hymns' programme in which one person talks about his or her life and chooses all the hymns and religious music in the programme.

But, in my view, the very high standards of the production team – and of all those from film department, outside broadcast department and planning who provide the complex back-up facilities for us – is only a part of the story!

Just as important is the effort that you, the people who 'star' in our programmes, put in week by week.

It looks simple enough on the screen; an introduction from Geoffrey Wheeler, a church full of people singing favourite hymns, and a half-dozen or so people talking about their lives and the way in which their faith in God has helped them. The reality is very different.

A BBC cameraman carefully notes new instructions on his shooting script for Songs of Praise at Coverack, Cornwall.

How it all starts

It all begins when somebody, somewhere writes to us with a letter, which usually begins:

'Dear Mr Murray, I saw your name on the end of last night's Songs of Praise, and thought you would be interested in coming to St John's because next year we are celebrating our anniversary/ our rector is retiring after fifty years/our new church is being opened' or any one of a dozen other reasons.

I write back sending them one of our fact sheets. This is a small leaflet which explains in great detail just how the programme is made and what kind of effort is required from each community.

If the local churches feel, after reading this, that they can cope with us, then we will put them on our waiting list.

I suppose we get fifty or sixty times as many invitations as we can ever hope to use. But everyone goes on the file, and we try to share the programmes out around the country so that every county receives a visit from us in due course.

Once the series producer has decided on the location, he will visit the town, meet as many of the local clergy as possible and help set up a steering committee to cope with the programme on the spot. He will also visit all the suitable churches and choose the one which he thinks will work best.

For example, we want to invite as many people as possible and we bring with us for the recording a large number of camera vans, electricity generators, a mobile control room, lights, cameras, scaffolding and other equipment – so we need somewhere outside the church building to park all this equipment.

Finding the interviewees

Once a location has been found, the members of the steering committee are invited to nominate members of their congregations whom they feel might be suitable as interviewees. They supply full details of these people on our special nomination forms (we also ask them to tell us about their musical resources, such as brass bands or children's orchestras). These forms provide the basic information for one of our researchers, who will shortly visit the town and talk to everyone suggested in his or her search for people to interview.

Obviously everyone we talk to in this way cannot be included in the programme – which is often a great pity because our researchers meet so many wonderful people that the job of making the final selection is often very difficult.

The hymns in each programme

are chosen from those suggested by the interviewees and by the local steering committee. Most of the time people are able to have their first choice, but occasionally a hymn may have been sung in the programme the week before so we may use their second or third choice.

A cameraman's view of the massed choirs rehearsing for the Songs of Praise programme from the harbour at Coverack, Cornwall.

In the thousand odd editions of Songs of Praise which have been transmitted during the programme's lifetime nearly ten thousand beautiful hymns, many old favourites, some new, all of them much-loved, have been sung, so you can see how difficult it can be to avoid too much repetition, or how easy it could be to miss out a hymn which means everything to a particular interviewee, just because we've heard it before!

Those are some of the pitfalls we try hard to avoid, with some success, and helped by our library of almost two hundred different hymn-books and the expertise of the Revd Michael Armitage, who has been the programme's music advisor for almost three years.

As soon as the hymns have been chosen we print a small hymnbook and the local community start their rehearsals. A keen conductor will hold at least three full rehearsals before we turn up with our equipment. One of the Songs of Praise producers will visit the rehearsals in order to listen to the music, to offer advice and to start thinking about the best way to use the music in the programme.

About now one of our film directors is also busy visiting those who will be taking part in the programme to make final arrangements for the filming of their interviews.

Sometimes, if the filming involves a visit to a hospital, school or factory, there can be considerable organisation required to obtain permission to film from the appropriate authority.

Behind the scenes

Meanwhile the engineering manager responsible for planning the technical aspects of the Outside Broadcast recording will be liaising with the police, with the electricity board, with scaffolders, lighting contractors and all the other people involved behind the

scenes to make sure that everything is where it should be when it should be.

Our two separate operations, film and Outside Broadcast recording, are completely different. Filming involves a four-man crew plus two production people, and is done with small, lightweight equipment wherever the people are being filmed. We go to them.

For the Outside Broadcast recording, at which the hymn-singing is recorded on videotape, we go to the chosen church, and all those taking part in the singing will come to us. It is an enormous undertaking, with miles of cables, dozens of lights, four large cameras, sound equipment and thirty or forty technicians, electricians, cameramen and sound people.

Just before transmission the film stories and the hymns are edited together into the final programme. Details are sent to the *Radio Times* and to the newspapers, and a copy of the programme is sent to the BBC Ceefax unit so that they can put the exact words of the hymns and stories on the screen, for the benefit of those who are deaf – and, of course, those who like to sing along.

That's our side of the operation. The rest is up to you, to those taking part. Songs of Praise belongs not only to those who make it but to those who appear in it, and equally to those who watch it week by week.

Watching it is, I hope, a pleasure; making it is very hard work and lots of fun. Singing on the programme is also very hard

The conductor rehearses the choir at Croydon Parish Church, London.

work. It is hard because everyone wants to get their bit right.
The conductor wants the singing and the playing right!
The producer wants everything right!
The lighting director wants his lighting right!
The cameramen want their pictures right!
The sound men want their balance right!
Those doing the singing want to get their voices right!

A lot of elements combine together to get one programme right. I'm glad to say most of the time we manage between us to get most of it right – but it takes a lot of hard work.

What's it for?

Well, that's how we make the programme – but what's it for?

Part of the congregation at Croydon Parish Church.

What exactly is it?

Songs of Praise is a tv programme about the Christian life of one community, seen through the eyes of people from that community, and celebrated through the worshipping voices of many hundreds of people from that community joining together in a church to sing favourite hymns.

Our aims are to make the best possible tv programme, which will compare favourably in every way with any other programme on British television, but at the same time will be unashamedly, openly religious.

I think we have succeeded in achieving this in programmes from as far apart as the windswept Falkland Islands and the sun-kissed island of Cyprus; from the plains of northern Germany to the community church in Shanghai, China; from Liverpool's magnificent new cathedral with thousands of people to Crawley Down's tiny village church with less than three hundred; from ancient Durham to modern Billericay; and from the places in

Cameraman at Carisbrooke Castle.

Jerusalem where Jesus walked to the medieval splendours of York Minster.

For many this programme has been a beacon of light in a world where religion and the organized churches are coming to mean less and less; for others it's a cheerful sing-song on Sunday evenings; for some – handicapped or housebound – it is their only chance of sharing in worship with other people.

For those working on it, the

The abiding impression left after watching Songs of Praise is the joy of so many of the people taking part – both singers and interviewees.

programme provides an opportunity to meet some of the nicest people in these and other lands, to be part of an ongoing success story, and a chance to put their work, whether they do it for God or man, in front of you every week.

For us this book is a permanent way of sharing with you some of the joy that we have been privileged to experience during the past few years with Songs of Praise, and to remind you again of some of the wonderful people we have met.

A weekly miracle

Sometimes we hear the criticism that churches are only full because we are there; that people would not come out unless 'the telly people' were at the church. It is, of course, perfectly true that when we visit a church it is usually full – but that is only because there will be worshippers there from many churches who, if they were not taking part in Songs of Praise, would still be at church.

Sometimes there are people from

ten churches, sometimes thirty, sometimes – as was the case on the Isle of Wight recently – worshippers from over 180 different churches taking part in the singing. In ecumenical terms a weekly minor miracle!

May I just finish by telling you of my trip to Coventry Cathedral last November for our Remembrance Sunday programme. Because of an industrial dispute, our cameras were unable to come. The people of Coventry knew that we would not be recording their singing, but

the cathedral was still full. And everyone sang those beautiful hymns with just as much feeling and fervour as if the cameras had been there.

Standing in the semi-darkness of that great cathedral, surrounded by hundreds and hundreds of Christians singing beautifully, made me realise once again what a pleasure and a privilege working with and for you has been.

God Bless you all.

Jim Murray

Jim Murray, producer of Songs of Praise.

Morning and Evening Hymns

Morning has broken

Until one Monday night a year ago, Geoffrey Bowling's life seemed very straightforward. He and his wife Ingrid had a beautiful house and two children they were proud of. . .

My son was sixteen. He was a fitness fanatic. He tried to do sixty press-ups in a minute on the Saturday, and he was just four short. In the evening we all went to a party at the badminton club. He had just had flu and wasn't quite himself. On Sunday he didn't feel too bad, but on the Monday he stayed home from school. My wife stayed at home to be with him. Suddenly at about 3.30 he said, 'Mum, I do feel really bad. I've got a terrible headache.' She gave him two tablets and thought he had gone to sleep.

We weren't worried. The doctor we'd called out the previous night had assured us that the temperature of 104 degrees was only flu. I went up at about half-past five and thought: 'There's something wrong: he's not asleep.' He was in a coma, deeply unconscious.

The doctor rushed round, an ambulance came, he was rushed into hospital, and by 9.30 he was dead.

We were devastated. At that time we didn't really know the cause. I shall never forget it. We came home to this house. We obviously couldn't sleep. We were just numb.

That was the longest night of my life. I asked myself: 'Why?' Then I started blaming: was it my fault? What could I have done? No, it was the doctor's fault, he didn't seem to come as quickly as he could. And then I thought no, it's God's fault. I've loved him all my life and this is what he does to me. There's no such thing as God. I looked on the bedside cabinet at the sleeping pills the doctor had left. And I could have taken them.

In that instant it was as if I heard Chris' voice in my head saying, 'Don't, dad, don't get bitter. Illness is an evil God wants us to fight.' It was as if I heaved a sigh of relief and realised that God was there. I felt an extraordinary peace. I would try and live as Chris would have wanted me to.

Geoffrey Bowling is a headmaster in Taunton, Somerset.

Morning has broken
Like the first morning,
Blackbird has spoken
*   Like the first bird.*
*   Praise for the singing!*
*   Praise for the morning!*
*   Praise for them, springing*
*   Fresh from the Word!*

Sweet the rain's new fall
Sunlit from heaven,
Like the first dewfall
*   On the first grass.*
*   Praise for the sweetness*
*   Of the wet garden,*
*   Sprung in completeness*
*   Where his feet pass.*

Mine is the sunlight!
Mine is the morning
Born of the one light
*   Eden saw play!*
*   Praise with elation,*
*   Praise every morning,*
*   God's re-creation*
*   Of the new day!*
Eleanor Farjeon

Olwyn Douglas never went to church. But her daughter Gillian was getting married . . .

New Every Morning

Olwyn used to think church was only for well-to-do people.

We thought we'd better go up to Christchurch and see what it was all about. We were just going to go the once. But then I wanted to go more, so we kept on going.

After a bit I joined a prayer group and I used to sit and say nothing at all – just listen. I thought it rather strange, people praying and asking God for things. I thought 'When I get home I'm going to try this.' But nothing happened, so I thought 'I know why it isn't happening. You have to be posh or clever. I do believe in God, but it doesn't seem he's taking any notice of me.'

But then Good Friday came, and there was a beautiful cross. When I looked at the cross I realised that Jesus loved me for what I was, not because I was clever or anything. It didn't change me, like my looks or outside, but it's all inside in my heart that I feel I've been changed.

I used to think the church was just for well-to-do people, well-dressed people and all that. I've lost all that feeling now. I think sometimes the church was to blame for things like that; but if people realise what Easter means, they realise it is for everybody.

I've chosen 'New every morning'. I must have sung it thousands of times at school, and it never had any meaning for me at all. But now when I wake up in the morning I say 'Thank you Lord for my night's rest', and I say this hymn as a prayer. When I was working, I used to say it over and over again on the way to work.

Olwyn Douglas worked for years in the pottery industry in Burslem, one of the famous 'five towns' of Arnold Bennett's novels.

Longton in Staffordshire is a pottery town, distinctive for its 'bottle' kilns, now largely superseded.

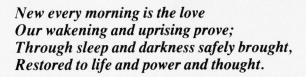

New every morning is the love
Our wakening and uprising prove;
Through sleep and darkness safely brought,
Restored to life and power and thought.

New mercies, each returning day,
Hover around us while we pray;
New perils past, new sins forgiven,
New thoughts of God, new hopes of heaven.

If on our daily course our mind
Be set to hallow all we find,
New treasures still, of countless price,
God will provide for sacrifice.

The trivial round, the common task,
Will furnish all we need to ask,
Room to deny ourselves, a road
To bring us daily nearer God.

Only, O Lord, in thy dear love
Fit us for perfect rest above;
And help us, this and every day,
To live more nearly as we pray.
John Keble (1792–1866)

Dr Robert Runcie, the Archbishop of Canterbury, has always been a firm supporter of **Songs of Praise.** *But he also confesses to a great personal love of hymns and hymn-singing.*

The day thou gavest, Lord is ended

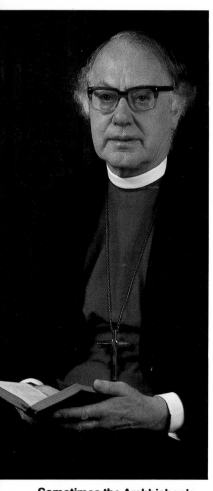

Sometimes the Archbishop's chaplain tells him not to sing too vigorously, for fear he use up all his energy!

I enjoy singing hymns. In fact I sometimes have to be restrained from singing them in services where I'm presiding, and chaplains whisper to me: 'Don't use up all your energy.' But I do get enthusiastic about hymns; I always look at the sort of hymns that have been chosen for any services in which I am to take part (and often interfere with the arrangements!).

I think that hymns have a very important part to play in worship, and I think *Songs of Praise* has an important part to play in communicating religious faith. I am proud of my association with the variation in the style of *Songs of Praise,* which enabled you to penetrate behind the singing faces to the little autobiographies of particular people. Because I think most people are influenced by the music which reminds them of special moments in their life, and people in their life.

That's what hymns mean to me – they remind me of particular places where I've somehow got closer to God, or God's perhaps drawn closer to me. If you said to me: 'Name six hymns,' I bet that immediately I would mention hymns which reminded me of rather special places or people. You know, the kind of hymn that was sung when I decided to be ordained, or when I met a particularly memorable Indian Christian years ago.

I'm not a musical connoisseur, you know. I have very popular tastes, and the hymn I would immediately choose is one that many other people would name – I'm sorry not to be more original – it's: 'The day thou gavest, Lord, is ended.' This has always been a favourite of mine; I've been fortunate enough to travel all over the world and whenever I'm singing that hymn, I can picture lots of different people of lots of Christian traditions – perhaps Indians in Bangalore or Chinese – with whom I have worshipped. It's never a tired or stale hymn. It's always fresh to me.

Lambeth Palace, on the River
Thames, is the official London
residence of the Archbishop of
Canterbury.

The day thou gavest, Lord, is ended,
  The darkness falls at thy behest;
To thee our morning hymns ascended,
  Thy praise shall sanctify our rest.

We thank thee that thy Church unsleeping,
  While earth rolls onward into light,
Through all the world her watch is keeping,
  And rests not now by day or night.

As o'er each continent and island
  The dawn leads on another day,
The voice of prayer is never silent,
  Nor dies the strain of praise away.

The sun that bids us rest is waking,
  Our brethren 'neath the western sky,
And hour by hour fresh lips are making,
  Thy wondrous doings heard on high.

So be it, Lord; thy throne shall never,
  Like earth's proud empires, pass away;
Thy kingdom stands, and grows for ever,
  Till all thy creatures own thy sway.

J. Ellerton (1826–93)

Abide with me

Margaret Chadd suffered the unbelievably cruel double-blow of losing two sons in two years. Facing that experience with faith and a lot of hard work, she now gives much of her time to helping people similarly bereaved.

When people ask me what family I have, it's a tricky question – and it also re-opens a terrible wound. I had four sons. The eldest, Christopher, was drowned on his godfather's yacht, *Morning Cloud,* in 1974 when he was twenty-three. Then, two years later, our third son, Timothy, who was up at Cambridge, was killed by a woman in a car when he was crossing the road on holiday in France.

You never think these things are going to happen to you, and when they do, the first impact is shock, numbness. Then the numbness wears off, and you're faced with the reality of it, which gives place to anger, against God perhaps – 'Why me?' – or guilt – 'Could I have prevented it?'

As time goes on, the pain lessens, and with the support of friends and family and one's own Christian faith one has the feeling that life has to go on for the sake of the members of the family who are left. One just has to pick up the pieces and re-make a jigsaw, realising that the pattern will never be complete again.

What we did was to find an old seventeenth-century

derelict farmhouse, where no-one had lived for fourteen years, and decided to restore it and make a new home. Most of our friends thought it was a mad idea, but we took it as a challenge. We have now achieved our new home, and from a wilderness created a garden in memory of our two sons. This entailed a lot of physical energy, but I found it very therapeutic.

I was fortunate in having other interests outside the home which required mental energy, and these included my work as a magistrate and with the Red Cross. Then I became involved with 'Compassionate Friends', who are parents who have lost a child and support each other; and later with 'Cruse', the organisation for the bereaved, that offers counselling, practical help and opportunity for social contact to those who need support during berevement. I was able to initiate the formation of a branch in Suffolk so that those who live alone or have no family support can share their feelings of anger or guilt with someone who is prepared to listen or receive help with practical problems such as housing or finance.

After losing two of her sons in a short period of time, Margaret Chadd moved to a farmhouse near Beccles, Suffolk.

Death in our society is an embarrassment to many people, isn't it? We don't have death rituals any more, and people don't know what is expected of them. I think it was a definite help when Mrs Snooks wore a black armband, the curtains were drawn, and people saw relatives die in their own home. Very often today they never see a dead body, just a coffin, and it's hard to come to terms with realising that the person has died. The mind shuts it out and pretends it hasn't happened.

The prayer that has helped me most and given me the greatest comfort in time of need is that of Father Bede

Mrs Chadd created a garden in memory of her two sons.

Jarrett:

We seem to give them back to thee, O God, who gavest them to us. Yet as thou didst not lose them by giving, so we have not lost them by their return. Not as the world gives do you give, O Lover of souls. What you give you do not take away, for what is yours is ours always, if we are yours. And life is eternal and love is immortal and death is only an horizon and an horizon is nothing save the limit of our sight.

When you are bereaved, you are left with a scar that you have to learn to live with. It may heal, but you'll never be quite the same person again. My Christian faith has helped me to cope, and I have chosen the hymn 'Abide with me' because, like so many people when they're newly bereaved, I had great difficulty sleeping, and some of the verses of this hymn seemed to meet my need.

Abide with me; fast falls the eventide:
The darkness deepens; Lord, with me abide:
When other helpers fail, and comforts flee,
Help of the helpless, O abide with me.

Swift to its close ebbs out life's little day;
Earth's joys grow dim, its glories pass away;
Change and decay in all around I see:
O thou who changest not, abide with me.

I need thy presence every passing hour;
What but thy grace can foil the tempter's power?
Who like thyself my guide and stay can be?
Through cloud and sunshine, Lord, abide with me.

I fear no foe with thee at hand to bless;
Ills have no weight, and tears no bitterness.
Where is death's sting? Where, grave, thy victory?
I triumph still, if thou abide with me.

Hold thou thy cross before my closing eyes;
Shine through the gloom, and point me to the skies:
Heaven's morning breaks, and earth's vain shadows flee;
In life, in death, O Lord, abide with me.
H. F. Lyte (1793–1847)

Hymns for Holy Week and Easter

Having contracted that very disabling disease, Multiple Sclerosis, Michael Frobisher found his life increasingly restricted. Here, he and his wife Pat describe how they cope with day-to-day living, and how Mike has directed his energies into a new interest.

There is a green hill

Michael Frobisher is a keen radio 'ham'. His wife Pat helps by writing up the log of his calls each day.

One of the main difficulties is that I can wake up in the morning and never know exactly how I'm going to feel that day, whether even I shall be able to talk the way I could the day before. Of course, I had to stop work, and, secondly, I had to stop driving the car.

I'm not mobile at all now; I have to rely on my wheel-chair for everything. And I'm fortunate in that I've got a hoist, so that I'm able now to go from my wheel-chair downstairs up to the bedroom, across the bed, and so to lying on the bed.

But one of the compensations, of course, is that now I'm at home all day long, I can operate the radio most of the time. I became interested in amateur radio quite a long time ago, but it wasn't until I contracted MS that I had the time to get involved. Then I was able to take the exam and become a qualified radio amateur.

I encouraged Michael to do it because I think it's a very good thing for someone who is in the house all day: it opens the world and he 'meets' new friends every morning. We have to have Michael downstairs by 8.15 no matter what, even if the boys are playing holy heck when they're dressing him, because he starts with one group then who are all travelling into Leeds, and they all chat away while he is having his breakfast. It's a Home Office rule that all the calls have to be logged, and of course Michael can't write, so he tapes all the calls he's done, and then I write them up at night.

I have to rely on the family a lot. The boys have to help me get dressed and undressed, and some days my hands are bad, and they have to cut my food up, so I can use just one hand.

I hate to be so dependent on other people, and that makes me very depressed. In fact depression would be an understatement at times; I find that the best thing then is take myself to bed – or rather somebody else takes me to bed – and I stay up there and get it all out of my system. But I get over it; I'm fortunate that I have a wife and family that are able to cope with my ups and

It was only after he contracted MS that Michael became seriously interested in amateur radio, and qualified as an operator.

downs. (You find that an awful lot of people with MS, their marriages have broken up.) And my depressions don't last long; I bounce back.

Let's be straight. In a family where there is any kind of chronic illness, there's bound to be a lot of tension and, in this household, the way of dealing with it is to explode! Michael shouts at the boys, I shout at him and the boys, everybody shouts. The dog goes and hides under the table. But it's our way of salvation really.

I get depressed too, and I can't go round with a long face. So I use the cathedral and St Marks a good deal. I slope in there just for a few minutes, get a sort of injection, and come out again usually feeling very much better. My eldest son was in the choir at the cathedral, and the hymn I have chosen, 'There is a green hill far away', was the piece that he had to sing at his audition.

There is a green hill far away,
*   Without a city wall,*
Where the dear Lord was crucified,
*   Who died to save us all.*

He died that we might be forgiven,
*   He died to make us good,*
That we might go at last to heaven,
*   Saved by his precious blood.*

There was no other good enough
*   To pay the price of sin;*
He only could unlock the gate
*   Of heaven, and let us in.*

O dearly, dearly has he loved,
*   And we must love him too,*
And trust in his redeeming blood,
*   And try his works to do.*
Cecil Frances Alexander (1818–95)

Rock of ages

Almost forty years ago, Elsie Noel's husband, brother and cousin were drowned in a lifeboat disaster. Today she works to support the lifeboat service, and to befriend families who have suffered a similar loss.

As it happened, my husband and I were the steward and stewardess of the British Legion Club, and he rang me round about tea-time to say that he'd been called out in the lifeboat. So I went up to the club to take over, because in those days we used to run old-time dances that went on till 11 o'clock.

Afterwards we locked up, but he still wasn't back. I walked down over the main road, and the lights were still on. I knew they hadn't come back.

I came home and made my supper. I waited and waited. Eventually I must have dropped off to sleep. About 5 o'clock I woke my son and said, 'Your father hasn't come home. Will you go and see what's the matter?'

An hour and a half later he came back. I happened to be in the window, and I watched him coming along the terrace and he said to me, 'Mum, they've found the boat upturned. I'm afraid dad is lost.' That's the memory I carry along all these years.

The day of the funeral it rained and rained. It was a terrible time. My brother was lost, my cousin was lost, and there were a lot of widows younger than me. The village was shocked, because it was just after the war had ended; all these men had come home to start a new life with their wives and children. That's why I keep in contact with the other disasters – I've spoken to the widows of the Penlee lifeboat, I've rung them up and written to them.

I was a long time getting over the tragedy. I often used to ask 'Why?'. You lose your grip that you had on your religion and life. Your faith is crushed sometimes, but I'm sure that it is there and it has to come to the surface again.

I go into the lifeboat house and talk to the crew. I hide my feelings, but if ever they go out during the night and the light is still on, I think: 'They're not back.'

I have chosen the hymn 'Rock of ages'. I remember my mother singing this to me when the boat went out with my father on board.

Elsie Noel.

Rock of ages, cleft for me,
Let me hide myself in thee;
Let the water and the blood,
From thy riven side which flowed,
Be of sin the double cure:
Cleanse me from its guilt and power.

Not the labours of my hands
Can fulfil thy law's demands;
Could my zeal no respite know,
Could my tears for ever flow,
All for sin could not atone:
Thou must save, and thou alone.

Nothing in my hand I bring;
Simply to thy Cross I cling;
Naked, come to thee for dress;
Helpless, look to thee for grace;
Foul, I to the fountain fly;
Wash me, Saviour, or I die.

While I draw this fleeting breath,
When mine eyes are closed in death,
When I soar through tracts unknown,
See thee on thy judgement-throne;
Rock of ages, cleft for me,
Let me hide myself in thee.
Augustus Montague Toplady (1740–78)

When I survey

Bill Thurkettle was fourteen-and-a-half when he first went to work down a Durham mine. Here he remembers that day, and the life of the mining community he was brought up in.

I remember it very well. Me father shouted me up at quarter-past-two in the morning. We had a bite of breakfast, and away he went down the road, and I put my hand in his, just like a boy. I was worried all the way down, to wonder where I was coming to.

And then we got to the surface and I got me lamp. I felt proud because I was getting a lamp – just an ordinary oil lamp. There was no electric lights in them days down the pit. We got into the cage and it went down to bottom, 540 feet, and my heart just lifted like that. I was in another world. I was given the job at the trapdoor: it's a ventilating door, where you've just got to sit and open and close the door, and let the tubs come through.

The unmistakeable silhouette of a coalmine pithead at Sacriston, Durham, where Bill Thurkettle worked for many years.

What was your life like, spending so much of your time in darkness?
It was rather strange: the time went by very quick. Your eyes were very, very dim sometimes, until you got used to the darkness. Some places was very damp, well very wet as a matter of fact, and it was always cold.

How much were you paid?
My first pay, I had 9/3d to draw, and me mother gave us threepence for me pocket-money.

Has your faith ever been tested?
It was tested in 1951, when I was severely injured in the pit. I was drawing supports out of the mine. I got one half of the support withdrawn, and I went in to hang the chain onto the second half, when down came everything on top of me. I was left in darkness, partly covered in stone; and then my mate was just back by. He heard it, and he ran in and dragged me about a yard. Where I'd been lying, the whole place just caved in.

And I prayed and I prayed and I prayed – right till I got to the hospital, and after I came out of me operation. I prayed and I thanked God for what he'd done for me, and from that day that faith has held me.

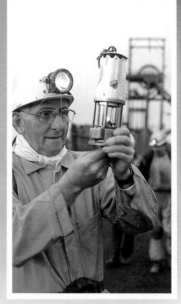

Bill Thurkettle remembers the days when there were no electric lamps down the mine.

When I survey the wondrous Cross
  On which the Prince of Glory died,
My richest gain I count but loss,
  And pour contempt on all my pride.

Forbid it, Lord, that I should boast
  Save in the Cross of Christ my God;
All the vain things that charm me most,
  I sacrifice them to his blood.

See from his head, his hands, his feet,
  Sorrow and love flow mingling down;
Did e'er such love and sorrow meet,
  Or thorns compose so rich a crown?

Were the whole realm of nature mine,
  That were an offering far too small;
Love so amazing, so divine,
  Demands my soul, my life, my all.

Isaac Watts (1674–1748) Based on Galatians 6:14

Nothing has made Winifred Darling's faith more real to her than a holiday spent in the Holy Land at Easter time.

This joyful Eastertide

It was a wonderful holiday. We spent it going through the Holy Land and, at Easter time, we were in Jerusalem where we visited the traditional sites.

But what really impressed me was when our Moslem guide took us to the site found by General Gordon. It was a green hill, just outside the city wall, and as I gazed on this hill, I thought: Golgotha, the green hill where Jesus was crucified. And I imagined the three crosses there, with Jesus crucified on the central cross, and at its foot Mary the mother of Jesus, and John, and the three women, and the soldiers casting their lots nearby.

The Mount of Olives, Jerusalem. The large church stands in the Garden of Gethsemane, and is known as the Church of the Nations.

Then he took us to a garden not very far away, and this really did impress me. It was the most beautiful place. Down one side of the garden was a sheer rockface and, at the bottom, there was a tomb that had been cut out of the rock, as the Gospel says. And I thought: this could be the place where Jesus was buried. And, when it was compared with the Gospel stories, it seemed to fit in. It was so still, so peaceful and so quiet; so shaded from the heat of the sun. The noise of the busy city didn't seem to penetrate into this garden, and, as I sat there in the stillness, I had a most reassuring experience – that Jesus really was alive. I felt it more than I'd ever felt it before. I felt as if I wanted to shout with joy. It was something that perhaps I'd been seeking most of my life.

So my choice of hymn is 'This joyful Eastertide'. The other reason I've chosen it is that it was always a favourite with my children at school – we sang it in the Easter services, and the little ones particularly did love the repetition in the chorus: 'Jesus is arisen, arisen, arisen'. They loved that part.

Winifred Darling visited the Garden Tomb in Jerusalem, which is similar to the rich man's tomb where Jesus was buried.

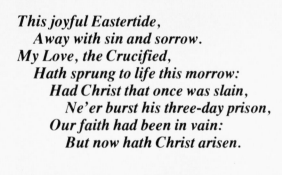

This joyful Eastertide,
    Away with sin and sorrow.
My Love, the Crucified,
    Hath sprung to life this morrow:
        Had Christ that once was slain,
          Ne'er burst his three-day prison,
        Our faith had been in vain:
          But now hath Christ arisen.

My flesh in hope shall rest,
    And for a season slumber:
Till trump from east to west
    Shall wake the dead in number:
        Had Christ, that once was slain, etc.

Death's flood hath lost his chill,
    Since Jesus crossed the river:
Lover of souls, from ill
    My passing soul deliver:
        Had Christ, that once was slain, etc.
G. R. Woodward

Right up to her hundredth birthday, Alice Sampson was living on her own, cooking and shopping for herself and walking to church on Sundays.

Jesus Christ is risen today

The distinctive steeple of the Cathedral dominates the skyline of Norwich, where centenarian Church Amy officer Alice Sampson now lives.

I was the eldest of eleven; there's a year and a half between me and the first sister, and, roughly speaking, two years between the others. But I think most of them are gone now. I'm trying to think.

Our mother saw that we learned our Sunday school lessons and our day school lessons too. As a family we wore out one Bible each year – Mother saw to it that we each read our portion to her every day, and those who didn't like reading had to come and sit by the table when mother was ironing and read to her then.

Then I joined the Church Army, because at that time I was hoping to be a missionary abroad. We had to wear

Jesus Christ is risen today,
    Alleluia!
Our triumphant holy day,
    Alleluia!
Who did once, upon the cross,
    Alleluia!
Suffer to redeem our loss.
    Alleluia!

black frocks with buttons down the front, fitted in round the waist, and cloaks and a little bonnet. A lot of people thought we were nurses!

Our job was mainly visiting people, the sick and the well and the babies – giving mothers advice, all sorts of things. We even used to help out and make the babies' nightdresses. And we would teach the children and play games with them – even go and play rounders in the school yard! Sometimes I would take a service, or had the children for instruction, and it just came naturally, I suppose, to talk about the Bible – as it should do. I wouldn't like to state that any part of our work was more important than another.

I couldn't tell you what is the secret of a long life – just living naturally I suppose. I've always liked walking – rarely used a bus. Perhaps part of the reason I am living longer is that I don't worry about tomorrow. I trust in God, and live for today. The only thing is, every day seems so short.

When she was dressed in her Church Army uniform, Alice Sampson was often mistaken for a nurse!

Hymns of praise then let us sing
  Alleluia!
Unto Christ, our heavenly King,
  Alleluia!
Who endured the cross and grave,
  Alleluia!
Sinners to redeem and save.
  Alleluia!

But the pains that he endured,
  Alleluia!
Our salvation have procured;
  Alleluia!
Now above the sky he's King,
  Alleluia!
Where the angels ever sing.
  Alleluia!

Lyra Davidica (1708) and others

Thine be the glory

Although he is a clergyman, John Lister, Provost and Vicar of Wakefield, finds that Easter has for him a much more personal relevance than a mere religious festival.

The Easter Day which I remember particularly was after the Coventry blitz. I'd never experienced anything in the way of suffering until then. I'd had a very happy life, been very fit, never known a day's illness. And then I was smashed up in the blitz – I had the doubtful privilege of being the first person on whom a landmine more or less descended. I was put out of action and blinded.

Before he retired, John Lister was Provost and Vicar of Wakefield, Yorkshire.

Having recovered from that, with my sight partially restored, I was ordained a priest, and two days later my sight went completely. Back into hospital just in time for the second Coventry blitz. After that, and a nursing home in Leamington, I was taken home to Worcester, absolutely shot up on Easter Eve – frightened and terrified, and with the added knowledge that my father was dying and I was responsible for my mother. It looked as though I would be able to do no job at all, and it seemed like the end of the world.

That was Easter Day. In the evening I listened to the service on the wireless. I can't remember much about it but, after it was over, I just knew I was going back to Coventry, I was going on with my work. I was told by the doctors that it would be a miracle if I ever saw to read again, and I have been reading regularly for years and years. I was told I wouldn't be able to work for two years, and I was back in my parish in three weeks!

So Easter really was Easter then – my own kind of resurrection in a way, but a resurrection which came from God not from myself. This was the tremendous

Easter Day means something very special to the Revd John Lister.

Although for a time completely blinded by a landmine, John Lister has now been reading regularly for years.

thing, because I'm still the sort of person who's terrified of going to the dentist, you know, that sort of thing.

With that miracle Easter at the back of my mind, my choice of hymn is 'Thine be the glory, risen conquering King', because it speaks of the power that God can give, and no-one else can give, through the personal power of Christ.

Thine be the glory, risen, conquering Son,
Endless is the victory thou o'er death hast won;
Angels in bright raiment rolled the stone away,
Kept the folded grave clothes where thy body lay.
   Thine be the glory, risen, conquering Son,
   Endless is the victory thou o'er death has won.

Lo, Jesus meets us, risen from the tomb;
Lovingly he greets us, scatters fear and gloom;
Let the church with gladness hymns of triumph sing,
For her Lord now liveth, death hath lost its sting.

No more we doubt thee, glorious Prince of Life;
Life is nought without thee: aid us in our strife;
Make us more than conquerors through thy deathless love;
Bring us safe through Jordan to thy home above.
E. L. Budry (1854–1932) tr. R. B. Hoyle (1875–1939)

God: Creator, Ruler, Father

Working as a Church Army evangelist in Wormwood Scrubs Prison, Edwin Bates feels that his parish is just like any other, except that it is bounded by walls.

Father, Lord of all Creation

The Church Army was set up from the very beginning to work with people who are perhaps pushed out by society, and, of course, prisoners are this sort of outcast group – society has locked them away. We accept that punishment is necessary – society must protect itself from people who, for instance, burgle houses – but while the men are here, we try to help make sure they don't come back again. I think it's trying to help them find something that they are looking for. My job is to introduce people to God, because I do believe that people are empty, if you like.

I'm not at all a Bible-punching sort of person; I never go round preaching to people. I try and create relationships, win trust, through talking to the men on very ordinary sorts of topics. And hopefully, through my own

Battersea power station dominates this view of South London.

Father, Lord of all Creation,
Ground of Being, Life and Love;
Height and depth beyond description
Only life in you can prove:
You are mortal life's dependence:
Thought, speech, sight are ours by grace;
Yours is every hour's existence,
Sovereign Lord of time and space.

example of being here and trying to show something of our Lord's love and compassion, they will see me putting the Christian gospel into practice. Sometimes the sort of person and his background is quite repugnant, and he's very difficult to like. But I try to love as Christ loved, to do something positive, and show concern for his situation.

Basically, I visit the men in their cells, discussing all sorts of problems, or just passing the time of day. On top of that, I do quite a lot of contacting of families, mostly by phone, just to keep in touch, or to let them know if the post's been delayed, something like that. Then we run evening groups and all sorts of activities similar to those in any outside church and, of course, there are our many chapel services.

My choice of hymn is 'Father, Lord of all creation'. It reminds me, especially working here, that ultimately, when God created this world, man was perfect, in the image of God. Somewhere along the line, we've fallen short of this, but the hymn gives me new hope that God can recreate – make people new.

Captain Edwin Bates believes his job is to introduce people to God.

Jesus Christ, the Man for Others,
*   We, your people, make our prayer:*
Give us grace to love as brothers
*   All whose burdens we can share.*
Where your name binds us together
*   You, Lord Christ, will surely be;*
Where no selfishness can sever
*   There your love may all men see.*

Holy Spirit, rushing, burning
*   Wind and flame of Pentecost,*
Fire our hearts afresh with yearning
*   To regain what we have lost.*
May your love unite our action,
*   Nevermore to speak alone:*
God, in us abolish faction,
*   God, through us your love make known.*

Copyright, Stewart Cross (b. 1928)

From jackaroo on an Australian sheepfarm to vicar of Cartmel, Lawrence Dykes has achieved a lot in his life. But he is even more proud of the achievements of his grandfather.

Holy, holy, holy!

Lawrence Dykes' grandfather J. B. Dykes wrote the tune of the hymn 'Lead Kindly Light' – and many others.

The musical correspondent of *The Times* once said that the finest tune in the whole of *Ancient and Modern* was 'Holy, holy, holy, Lord God Almighty', and it was written by an amateur. That amateur was J. B. Dykes, my grandfather, who was born in 1823. He was given a doctorate of music by the University of Durham because of the work he did in the cathedral. But he actually was an amateur who could write a tune.

He wrote the tune to one of the best-known hymns that has ever been, 'Lead kindly Light'. The words were written by Cardinal Newman, during a calm on the Red Sea. My grandfather was walking along the Strand, and suddenly the tune came to him. Some years later, there was a meeting in Chicago of all the religious sects in the world and the only thing they could agree on was saying the Lord's Prayer and singing 'Lead kindly Light'. Somebody turned to Cardinal Newman and said: 'You must be proud to think that the words of your hymn have gone all over the world.' He said: 'They wouldn't have gone all over the world except for Dykes' tune.'

And, wherever seamen meet in this world, they sing 'Eternal Father strong to save'. When Kennedy went to his grave, that was the tune they played. And when the *Titanic* went down, the tune they were playing was 'Nearer my God to Thee', by J. B. Dykes!

I have chosen the hymn, 'Holy, holy, holy! Lord God Almighty', not only because my grandfather wrote the tune, but, more than that, when I sing it, I see a vision of the world that is to be, or more exactly, the world that already is: if the Resurrection and Ascension are true, then all the problems facing the world have already been solved.

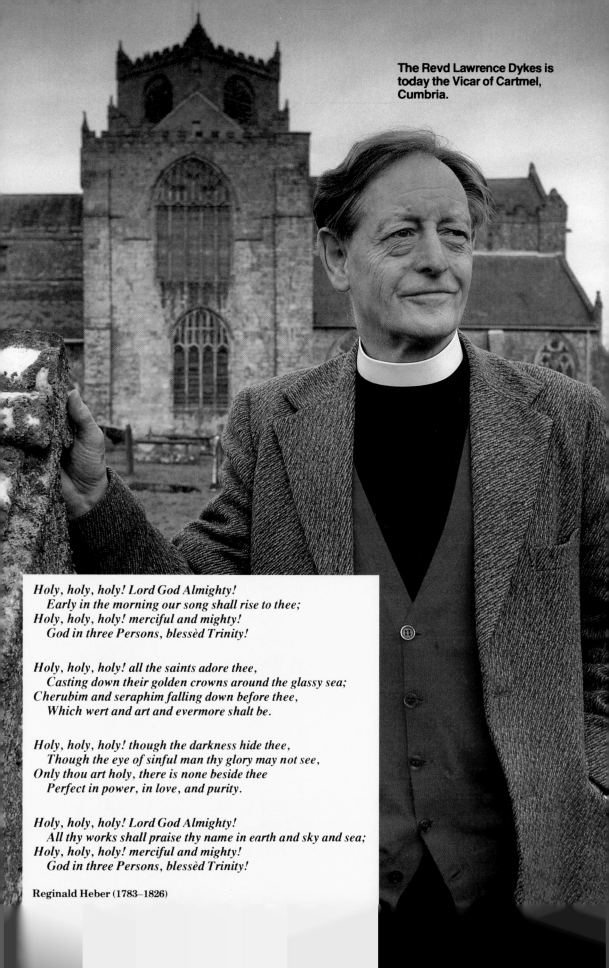

The Revd Lawrence Dykes is today the Vicar of Cartmel, Cumbria.

Holy, holy, holy! Lord God Almighty!
  Early in the morning our song shall rise to thee;
Holy, holy, holy! merciful and mighty!
  God in three Persons, blessèd Trinity!

Holy, holy, holy! all the saints adore thee,
  Casting down their golden crowns around the glassy sea;
Cherubim and seraphim falling down before thee,
  Which wert and art and evermore shalt be.

Holy, holy, holy! though the darkness hide thee,
  Though the eye of sinful man thy glory may not see,
Only thou art holy, there is none beside thee
  Perfect in power, in love, and purity.

Holy, holy, holy! Lord God Almighty!
  All thy works shall praise thy name in earth and sky and sea;
Holy, holy, holy! merciful and mighty!
  God in three Persons, blessèd Trinity!

Reginald Heber (1783–1826)

Major Martin Amlot was interviewed for Songs of Praise in the middle of a Nato training exercise in Germany.

Dear Lord and Father of mankind

In the late part of the twentieth century we live in a Christian society in Britain and the army is part of that society, and the values which that society has, the laws, the ethics of that society, are reflected in the army. The military virtues of loyalty, courage, discipline and service are the Christian virtues. It's just that the greater panorama of faith as well adds a great deal more meaning to it than just the military virtues.

We're a compassionate army. We're as likely to be involved in disaster relief as involved in any kind of fighting. Although I've served in Northern Ireland, the Northern Ireland experience has certainly not been as large as my experience on disaster relief and operations of a compassionate nature.

In my view it is important to present my soldiers with every opportunity to find the strength that I've found through a Christian faith, so that my company they know jolly well that I'm interested and that I take my Christianity and my faith seriously. But at the same time I know that I could put them off and that they wouldn't come anywhere near a church and they wouldn't take my views seriously at all if I oversold them. Certainly I believe I've a role in setting an example, in setting a lead which they can choose or choose not to follow.

I've travelled widely, obviously, in the army, all over the world. I've seen many countries and both of us, Jaki my wife and I, know jolly well that we're happiest back in England. But the way of life, the values and the laws and the system in England, are things which we cherish, and in terms of being a soldier are prepared to do a great deal to defend.

The hymn I've chosen is, 'Dear Lord and Father of mankind'. It's a super hymn. It's a hymn about praise as a good hymn should be. It's a hymn about duty and a hymn about service too. A particular line I like is 'Take from our souls the strain and stress . . .'. We're in a stressful business, we work hard . . . (we think we work hard!), we play hard, but we all look forward to and enjoy the quiet times too. This hymn talks about that. But it talks principally about peace, and if we're not in the peace business then who is? And I like the sentiments of striving for peace and the general sentiments throughout the hymn of worship and peace and duty and praise. I like the hymn. It's got a good tune too, and that's important.

Major Amlot believes he should set a lead by his Christian faith, which his soldiers can choose, or choose not, to follow.

Warminster, Wiltshire. Much of the surrounding countryside is used by the Army for training and exercises.

Presenting Songs of Praise

'Hello? Geoffrey? Songs of Praise office here. Can you do a programme three weeks on Thursday at . . .?'

The beginning is always the same – the telephone call or the letter – but the last part is always different. It could be anywhere, from Fort William to Folkestone, Cirencester to Cyprus. Perhaps a national beauty spot or a run down inner-city area; but, wherever it is, it will be fascinating – absolutely fascinating.

'Old Style'

There have been two kinds of *Songs of Praise* programmes, sharing the same title, and based upon a group of people singing their favourite hymns, but otherwise very different indeed. In what we now call the 'old style' programme, my work began soon after the telephone booking. By the next morning's post would arrive a guidebook of the church, together with a list of the hymns in their running order. The shelves of my study bend under the weight of gazeteers, books of history, of legends of the derivation of ancient place names, as well as the hymn books of just about every Christian sect and denomination. Lives of saints, guides to cathedrals, road maps and books that councils publish about their towns and cities. These were the quarries from which was cut the material for the links.

The 'links'

In the early days the links – the introductions to the hymns – were fairly simple. 'Our next hymn was written by a man who used to live near here. He was quite famous for the lovely roses he used to grow . . .' – that kind of thing. Quite interesting, but not really helping the hymn writer to put across his message, especially when the words were being sung by several hundred people, and therefore not as clear as when spoken by just one.

Gradually the approach began to change. For me it began to change soon after I was licensed as a Reader at my own church. From that time, I was especially concerned to show that the famous people in local history, the individuals who lived and shared their lives with Jesus, about whom we read in the Bible, and the people around me in the church, as well as the others watching the programme at home, were all no more nor less than human beings. They are separated by an accident of time into living different lives in different life-styles, but have every human characteristic, good and bad, in common.

It was to people just like these the Jesus actually spoke, and that St. Paul spoke *about* Jesus and his teaching. Hymn-writers like the Wesleys had, in many instances, taken those words and that teaching and brilliantly condensed it into the verses of a hymn. My task, as I saw it, was simply to un-condense it, to

Geoffrey Wheeler prepares for an open-air interview at Coverack, Cornwall.

46

expand it, to re-constitute it, if you like, indicating the original saying and underlining its message.

The trouble with hymns is that it is very easy to sing them without really thinking or realising just what it is we are singing. I received many, many letters thanking me for what were often referred to as 'mini-sermons'. Well, the 'sermons' were not mine but Wesley's.

Once written, the links had to be memorised and delivered to camera in between the hymns. Not always easy, especially when, out of the corner of your eye, you saw a choir tiptoeing into position, or a camera getting stuck on a pew-end! The titles are often deceptively similar, too – 'Father', 'Lord', 'God', 'Christ' and 'Jesus' can easily be accidentally exchanged, and, as the title usually came at the end of the link, the whole thing had then to be done again.

When things go wrong

There were the times when things went wrong. On my way to a programme at Birkenhead, I was in a traffic jam in the middle of Liverpool. It was midsummer, and sweltering. Time went on and nothing moved. Switching on my radio, I heard that a furniture van had jammed its roof against the roof of the Mersey Tunnel – the one I was waiting to get through. I was stuck, without a hope of getting through the tunnel in time. When I tried to move my car out of the jam, drivers closed up, pretending not to see. Eventually, abandoning the car at the roadside, I ran to the underground railway and made it just in time for the first link.

Then there was the time at Sunderland. I was up in a high pulpit, where I'd been hoisted, as my left leg was in plaster following a skiing accident. Suddenly, an alarm – the control van had gone

Geoffrey Wheeler chats to some of the local Christians taking part in the Songs of Praise programme broadcast from Coverack, Cornwall.

Manaccan Parish Church, Cornwall.

on fire. 'Would the congregation evacuate the church as soon as possible?' They did, so did the crew, and I was left abandoned in a smoky pulpit!

'New Style'

The second kind of *Songs of Praise* programme is the present format – 'New Style' as it is known. In these we see members of the congregation, and then meet them, in filmed interview, doing their daily work, or at home, or wherever. These are the people who make the programmes so fascinating for me.

I love going to different places of course, but I love even more meeting the different people. Some I have spoken to have been very young, others very old, some had only weeks to live – and knew it. Some, inevitably, merge in the memory, but others remain clear and distinct, never to be forgotten: the young sergeant of the Light Infantry who was leading his platoon across the blistering heights of the Cyprus mountains, who thought of home and asked for 'Jerusalem' to remind him of England's green and pleasant land. And the great sound of the band, the mighty organ and a thousand voices that filled Durham Cathedral in response to his request. The old soldier who had gone to the trenches with five hundred others, and returned with fifteen, who, at ninety, remembered them still and asked for 'O Valiant Hearts' in their honour.

Some are great and famous people – the Archbishop of Canterbury and the Archbishop of Westminster discussing the impact of God upon the lives of people. Others are unknown and uncomplicated – the eleven-year-old Chinese girl speaking of the Holy Spirit 'popping out and hitting you on the nose!' He has done so

The Parish Church, St Keverne, Cornwall.

A recent Songs of Praise programme was made in China.

to me many times in the course of this series.

Songs of Praise is a wonderful programme – by that I mean a programme full of wonder. It is quite different from any other programme, because it is totally real. To be invited by people, week after week, to enter into their homes, and in some cases into their innermost lives, is a great privilege and a great joy. And joy is the feeling that comes through – in the interviews, in the singing of the hymns, and certainly in the many letters I receive from the millions who share our programme each week in their own homes. Is it any wonder that, as people tell me, I look happy when I say 'Good evening – and welcome to Songs of Praise'?

Geoffrey Wheeler.

David Kremer, one of the producers of Songs of Praise, watches the TV monitors with **programme assistant Liz Ryves-Brown during the recording of the programme.**

Geoffrey Wheeler in the Judean Hills, for an Easter programme.

Jesus Christ

And can it be

Born to an unhappy childhood in Jamaica, Rose Hudson finally discovered love through her adopted family and her faith in God. She now puts that love and faith into practice working for the Church Army.

Rose, what sort of family background did you have?
I come from a large family – three brothers and three sisters. One sister and I didn't live with our mother – she was here in England – and I grew up in Jamaica with my aunt, my father's sister. Then, when I was about ten, my mother decided she would take us to live with her. But that didn't work out at all well because we just didn't get on with her; my sister and I felt that she was very prejudiced to us, and that she didn't love us. You know, she loved my other sisters and brothers who were born here and their dad who she married to, but she didn't marry to our dad. There was a lot of bitterness and hatred. My sister and I felt as if we wanted to be loved by our mother, and we didn't get that, so we hated her for it, and we hated my younger brothers and sisters as well, because they were taking it away from us.

Rose Hudson trained at the Church Army college in Blackheath, London, before returning to the West Indies.

You grew up very short on love. Are you still?
I don't think I am now, fortunately. I have an adopted
mum and dad, and they were happy to offer me love, and
there is also the love that I'm receiving from God, which
plays just as important a part.

Can you explain that a bit more?
Well, during my teens I was still fighting about this
whole concept of love, not loving my parents, and them
not loving me, and my blaming them for it. And it was at
this time that a friend of mine from high school
informed me about this God of love. She spoke about
him in a personal way, and I wanted to know more about
him. I wanted love, and, if he was the God of love then
surely he could give me this love. So I received him there
and then – I suppose you could say I accepted this loving
faith.

*And has it been enough? You haven't felt the need to turn
to human love?*
I think there's a need to turn to human love in just the
same way; this love has got to be made tangible
somewhere along the line.

The Essex coast near Westcliff-on-Sea.

And can it be that I should gain
*   An interest in the Saviour's blood?*
Died he for me, who caused his pain?
*   For me, who him to death pursued?*
Amazing love! how can it be
That thou, my God, shouldst die for me!

'Tis mystery all! The Immortal dies:
*   Who can explore his strange design?*
In vain the first-born seraph tries
*   To sound the depths of love divine.*
'Tis mercy all! let earth adore,
Let angel minds inquire no more.

He left his Father's throne above –
*   So free, so infinite his grace –*
Emptied himself of all but love,
*   And bled for Adam's helpless race.*
'Tis mercy all, immense and free;
For, O my God, it found out me!

Long my imprisoned spirit lay
*   Fast bound in sin and nature's night;*
Thine eye diffused a quickening ray –
*   I woke, the dungeon flamed with light;*
My chains fell off, my heart was free,
I rose, went forth, and followed thee.

No condemnation now I dread;
*   Jesus, and all in him, is mine!*
Alive in him, my living Head,
*   And clothed in righteousness divine,*
Bold I approach the eternal throne,
And claim the crown, through Christ, my own.

Charles Wesley (1707–88)

Alan Thomas is a church architect. He feels that working with the fabric of our ancient churches not only brings him into touch with the craftsmen working there before him, but strengthens his own beliefs.

Lord of the Dance

People are often asked to give money for the upkeep and conservation of churches and cathedrals. Is this really worthwhile?
It certainly is. Apart from being our country's heritage, I believe the church buildings provide a continuity for the faith. The building of this cathedral eight hundred years ago indicated a massive confidence in the future.

Has working with churches influenced your own faith at all?
Oh yes, it has strengthened it and, in fact, has provided much of the evidence that I seem to require in my progress towards full belief.

Alan Thomas examines a piece of masonry from the roof of Wells Cathedral, Somerset.

You're dealing with the work of individual craftsmen who lived hundreds of years ago. Do you ever feel that you're getting to know them as people?

Yes, each building is quite likely only to have been worked on by a small team of masons and carpenters, and one can come to recognise the individual work. Occasionally one feels, well, they stopped for lunch here! The form of the buildings certainly lent itself to individual craftsmen expressing themselves. Even in the quiet places and dark corners, the craftsman has completed something to his satisfaction, as a prayer to God.

You have chosen as your hymn, 'Lord of the Dance'. Why?

It expresses the brightness of Easter, and the optimism, fun and hope for the future that I've found in my progress so far. I'm sure that the cathedral builders themselves often felt like this when they were working here.

Alan Thomas, who specialises in church architecture, has been closely involved in the restoration of Wells Cathedral.

I danced in the morning
    when the world was begun,
And I danced in the moon
    and the stars and the sun,
And I came down from heaven
    and I danced on the earth;
At Bethlehem
    I had my birth.

Chorus:
Dance then wherever you may be;
I am the Lord of the Dance, said he,
And I'll lead you all, wherever you may be,
And I'll lead you all in the dance, said he.

I danced for the scribe
    and the pharisee,
But they would not dance
    and they wouldn't follow me;
I danced for the fishermen,
    for James and John;
They came with me
    and the dance went on:

I danced on the Sabbath
    and I cured the lame:
The holy people
    said it was a shame.
They whipped and they stripped
    and they hung me high,
And they left me there
    on a cross to die:

I danced on a Friday
    when the sky turned black;
It's hard to dance
    with the devil on your back.
They buried my body
    and they thought I'd gone;
But I am the dance
    and I still go on:

They cut me down
    and I leap up high;
I am the life
    that'll never, never die;
I'll live in you
    if you'll live in me:
I am the Lord
    of the Dance, said he:

Sydney Carter (b. 1915)

A stray American bomb in 1944 started a life-long interest in stained glass for Guernseyman, Hedley Ogier.

Alleluia, sing to Jesus!

Hedley Ogier's interest in stained glass was greatly stimulated when an English artist came to Guernsey and set up a workshop.

The American Air Force were hunting a German submarine, and dropped the bomb in St Peter Port harbour. Unfortunately, the Germans had moved the submarine! The consequence of the blast was that ninety per cent of the glass in the town church was shattered.

My interest in stained glass and leadlights began in 1948 when I was sent along to put in some replacement glass. As the years progressed, I found myself fixing stained glass in island churches for many companies on the mainland, sometimes assisting others, and then doing some in my own way.

Finally, about twenty years ago, an experienced stained glass artist from England, Miss Mary Eily de Putron, took up residence on Guernsey and set up a small workshop. She had several commissions, and was looking for someone to help her on the benchwork, which is actually making stained glass leadlights, as opposed to just fixing them. So, after a crash-course by her glazier, who came over very kindly one weekend to give me the real know-how of working on the bench with the lights, I became her assistant. Together, we reglazed Trinity Church into a Wren-style glazing, and we have made leadlights for several of the island churches.

It is my humble pleasure to say that I have worked in probably every Anglican church in the island, bar one, and in quite a few of the other denominations. I found intense interest all the time that I have been doing this; it has given me a chance to follow a craft and also to be able to use my talents for the churches.

I've chosen as my hymn 'Alleluia, sing to Jesus', because the writer put down in words what I feel; that, in our sorrows, we are not alone if we really ask and ask in faith.

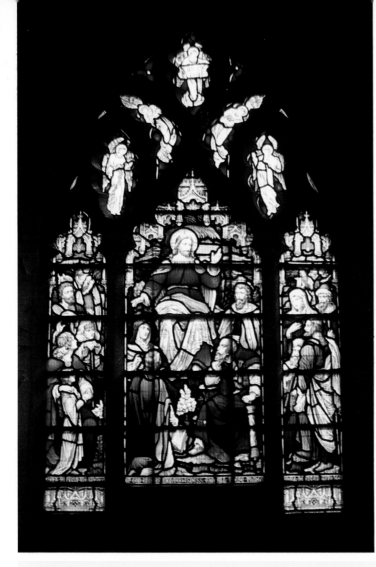

Stained glass from St Mary's,
Hornsey Rise, London.

Alleluia, sing to Jesus!
  His the sceptre, his the throne;
Alleluia, his the triumph,
  His the victory alone:
Hark, the songs of peaceful Sion
  Thunder like a mighty flood;
Jesus out of every nation
  Hath redeemed us by his blood.

Alleluia, not as orphans
  Are we left in sorrow now;
Alleluia, he is near us,
  Faith believes, nor questions how:
Though the cloud from sight received him,
  When the forty days were o'er,
Shall our hearts forget his promise,
  'I am with you evermore'?

Alleluia, bread of angels,
  Thou on earth our food, our stay;
Alleluia, here the sinful
  Flee to thee from day to day:
Intercessor, Friend of sinners,
  Earth's Redeemer, plead for me,
Where the songs of all the sinless
  Sweep across the crystal sea.

Alleluia, King eternal,
  Thee the Lord of lords we own;
Alleluia, born of Mary,
  Earth thy footstool, heaven thy throne:
Thou within the veil hast entered,
  Robed in flesh, our great High Priest,
Thou on earth both Priest and Victim
  In the eucharistic feast.

W. Chatterton Dix (1837–98)

When Graham Leaman was told that he was going to be made redundant, he felt that twenty years of his life were just disappearing.

O for a thousand tongues

I remember seeing the anxious faces of my friends and colleagues, and I began to feel very depressed and unhappy. And then I began to feel angry, perhaps a little resentful, and I found myself blaming others for what had happened. Then I realised that this was incompatible with my Christian life and character, and so I did something that might seem rather odd to people who aren't believers; my wife and I made it a matter of prayer, as we do with all our problems.

I didn't ask God to find me another job – I realised there were three million others who were looking for jobs too. But we did ask him to show us his will for our

Cross Keys, Gwent, nestles in the hills of South Wales.

lives, and I remember recalling the words of our annual covenant service: 'Put me to what thou wilt, rank me with whom thou wilt, put me to doing, put me to suffering, let me be employed for thee or laid aside for thee'. I tried to use that prayer.

I was certain that God would answer, and I believe he is. During that year I was asked if I would like some part-time teaching at a college of further education. This I gladly accepted, and it has led to a full-time, though temporary, job, teaching engineering to sixteen-year-old boys. I am finding this very satisfying; these boys can't find jobs either and, through my experience as an engineer and as being unemployed, and most of all, as a Christian, I believe that I can find a way of service.

I often find difficulty in finding words sufficient to praise God as I would like, and Charles Wesley has expressed this feeling in the hymn I have chosen, 'O for a thousand tongues to sing my great Redeemer's praise'.

Graham Leamon has found a satisfying new vocation teaching engineering to school-leavers.

> O for a thousand tongues to sing
>   My dear Redeemer's praise,
> The glories of my God and King,
>   The triumphs of his grace!
>
> Jesus! the name that charms our fears,
>   That bids our sorrows cease;
> 'Tis music in the sinner's ears,
>   'Tis life and health and peace.
>
> He speaks; and, listening to his voice,
>   New life the dead receive,
> The mournful broken hearts rejoice,
>   The humble poor believe.
>
> Hear him, ye deaf; his praise, ye dumb,
>   Your loosened tongues employ;
> Ye blind, behold your Saviour come;
>   And leap, ye lame, for joy!
>
> My gracious Master and my God,
>   Assist me to proclaim
> And spread through all the earth abroad
>   The honours of thy name.
>
> **Charles Wesley (1707–88)**

Taken prisoner by the Germans, Bill Sykes suffered a particularly rough time at the hands of the SS. He now believes that, if he met one of them face to face, he could forgive them.

Bill Sykes was sent to a special punishment camp for recalcitrant prisoners of war.

Come down, O Love divine

If orders given to me by the commandants of the various camps were contrary to the Geneva Convention, I refused to comply. Three times I attempted unsuccessfully to escape, and, on being recaptured, the sentence on each occasion, given after lengthy interrogation, was twenty-eight days' solitary confinement in an underground cell.

Following my third sentence, I was transported to a Strafe-lager (punishment camp) controlled solely by the SS. Here, because of my unwillingness to co-operate, I was subjected to flogging, given only bread and water once in three days, and had the backs of my hands dabbed with acid pads. It was painful, very painful.

I felt very bitter towards the SS. The one thought I had was to try and remember the faces of the ones who dealt out the most punishment and enjoyed doing it, just in case we ever came out on top.

After the war, my wife persuaded me to go along to a meeting that she and my daughter had attended the previous night. During the course of it a most extraordinary thing happened. An elderly lady confined to an invalid chair with severe arthritis, and whom I had often seen in the town, asked the minister to pray for her. He placed his hands on her head, offered a simple prayer, and continued with the service. The lady got up, walked out of the hall, and returned about thirty minutes later. She told us she had walked down two flights of stairs, and walked along the sea-front and back!

After the service we were invited to a private house, and during prayer I experienced a feeling of exultation which I have never been able to describe. I realised that the Holy Spirit had filled me, and that feeling has grown and grown in me from that time onwards.

So now I can honestly say that my feelings about the SS would be the reverse of what they were. I can't be absolutely certain what my reaction would be to such a meeting; but I know I would feel I had to forgive, to obey Christ's commandment to love one another.

My hymn choice is 'Come down, O Love divine', because I feel that, whatever may go wrong, the Comforter will present himself and say: 'Do not worry; I am with you'.

Come down, O Love divine,
Seek thou this soul of mine,
    And visit it with thine own ardour glowing;
O Comforter, draw near,
Within my heart appear,
    And kindle it, thy holy flame bestowing.

O let it freely burn,
Till earthly passions turn
    To dust and ashes in its heat consuming;
And let thy glorious light
Shine ever on my sight,
    And clothe me round, the while my path illuming.

Let holy charity
Mine outward vesture be,
    And lowliness become mine inner clothing;
True lowliness of heart,
Which takes the humbler part,
    And o'er its own shortcomings weeps with loathing.

And so the yearning strong,
With which the soul will long,
    Shall far outpass the power of human telling;
For none can guess its grace,
Till he become the place
    Wherein the Holy Spirit makes his dwelling.

Bianco da Siena, d. 1434. Tr. R. F. Littledale (1833–90)

Bill Sykes is churchwarden at his parish church in Suffolk.

Bill Sykes says that his feelings towards the SS have now been reversed.

Leaving Oxford University with a physics degree and then becoming a policeman is not a common path to follow. But Paul West did just that and finds his work even more fulfilling than he had hoped.

Love divine

The magnificent Cathedral at Durham, built over the shrine of St Cuthbert, broods over the city.

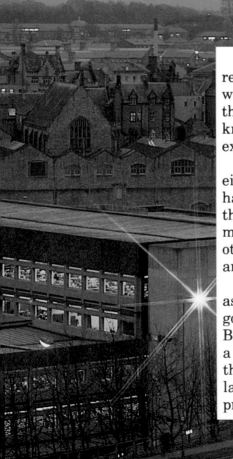

I wanted to be a policeman since I was about fifteen. I felt it was a really good public service; we're there all the time for people if anything happens to them, if anything goes wrong. I think most policemen derive an awful lot of satisfaction from being there in a helpful capacity.

We have an image of always being associated with unpleasant things; when we come to people's doors, everybody thinks something terrible must have happened. But often, if someone's car has been stolen or their house broken into, we can, with a bit of luck and a lot of hard work, recover stolen property and make people happy again.

Our job varies depending on whether it's night or day. During the day, police constables tend to walk around the streets as a presence for people to turn to if they need help – often we're asked for directions, we pop into shops, make sure everyone's alright and, obviously, in a town centre area, a lot of the time is taken up with traffic regulation.

At night-time there aren't many people about, so really all we do is look and listen for anything unusual, with a view to stopping burglaries and break-ins during the night hours. It can be boring at times, but you never know what's going to happen, and that keeps the excitement going.

We meet a lot of different people, but they tend to be either people who have had something unpleasant happen to them, or those who've done something wrong themselves. Generally we don't come across the normal members of society. I think that, unless we had any other beliefs, we could start to believe that the world is an even worse place than is pictured in the newspapers.

I've always had a Christian faith, which is marvellous as a policeman, because it makes you realise there is a good force in the world as well as an awful lot of evil. Before I joined the police force, I thought there might be a lot of conflict between my work and my faith – the thought of arresting somebody didn't seem a particularly Christian act. But then you realise that you are protecting people.

I believe God's love can flow through us all to reach other people if we only open our hearts and minds to let it happen. A lot of what we do, especially with regard to criminals, is unpleasant and if only we can discharge our activities with a bit more compassion and love towards our fellow men, that can make it more satisfying and worthwhile. Most people, even being arrested, are very dignified, and police officers act in a dignified manner.

Paul West wanted to be a policeman since about the age of fifteen.

Love divine, all loves excelling,
  Joy of heaven, to earth come down,
Fix in us thy humble dwelling,
  All thy faithful mercies crown.

Jesus, thou art all compassion,
  Pure, unbounded love thou art;
Visit us with thy salvation,
  Enter every longing heart.

Come, almighty to deliver,
  Let us all thy life receive;
Suddenly return, and never,
  Never more thy temples leave.

Thee we would be always blessing,
  Serve thee as thy hosts above,
Pray, and praise thee, without ceasing,
  Glory in thy perfect love.

Finish then thy new creation:
  Pure and spotless may we be;
Let us see thy great salvation,
  Perfectly restored in thee.

Changed from glory into glory,
  Till in heaven we take our place,
Till we cast our crowns before thee,
  Lost in wonder, love, and praise.

Charles Wesley (1707–88)

What a friend we have in Jesus

Arthur Rowlands was an ordinary police officer going about his routine duties when he was fired on at point-blank range by a man armed with a sawn-off shotgun. Today he is totally blind.

Caernavon Castle, North Wales.

It was 3am on Wednesday 2nd August 1961. I was not looking for a gunman. I just heard a noise and went to check. I came face to face with this person. When I challenged him, he pointed a gun and fired right into my face. I can still see him: I could give you his description today.

I was taken to hospital eighteen miles away, and from there to another hospital. When I came round and the consultant broke the news to me, I thought it was the end of the world. He said: 'You'll never see again. The man who shot you is the last person you'll ever see.' It was very, very black at that moment.

At first I felt very bitter, because that man had taken the most valuable thing in the world. I had a wife and

What a friend we have in Jesus,
All our sins and griefs to bear!
What a privilege to carry
Everything to God in prayer!
O what peace we often forfeit,
O what needless pain we bear,
All because we do not carry
Everything to God in prayer!

two young children; I was going to miss seeing them grow up. But time is a very good healer. I am far better off than him. Unfortunately he was not of a sound mind, and was given thirty years in Broadmoor. I bear no malice against him now.

My family and friends were behind me all the time. My wife is the best in the world; she stayed in the hospital and nursed me almost continuously. Your friends and family are your roots, planted deep so that you can withstand any storm that you meet. I feel there is a religious bearing in people: we should try to find Jesus Christ in other human beings. There are many good people in this world of ours.

When I left hospital, I was sent for a rehabilitation course at Torquay, and then to the Commercial College for the Blind in London. I trained as a telephonist so that I could return to civilian life as a communication operator with my own police force. I look at it as if I'm still carrying out my duties as any other police officer, trying to help the public to the best of my ability.

Although blinded by a gunman, Arthur Rowlands is still able to work for his own police force as a communication operator.

Have we trials and temptations?
  Is there trouble anywhere?
We should never be discouraged:
  Take it to the Lord in prayer.
Can we find a friend so faithful,
  Who will all our sorrows share?
Jesus knows our every weakness:
  Take it to the Lord in prayer.

Are we weak and heavy-laden,
  Cumbered with a load of care?
Precious Saviour, still our refuge:
  Take it to the Lord in prayer.
Do thy friends despise, forsake thee?
  Take it to the Lord in prayer;
In his arms he'll take and shield thee,
  Thou wilt find a solace there.

Joseph Medlicott Scriven (1820–86)

Shot down over Germany during the last war, Laurie Woolliscroft received a gift which touched him deeply and had far-reaching effects.

Hills of the North, rejoice

Laurie Woolliscroft has built a lasting friendship with German ex-prisoner of war Willie Bretsner.

I was standing in the weakest part of the aircraft when we were hit. The navigator pointed to my parachute on the floor. As I fastened the first hook, we exploded and I came spinning down sideways. I landed in some trees. I found myself praying harder than I'd ever prayed since childhood – not thanking God for saving me; just praying it was one of *my* crew in the other parachute which I saw falling through the sky. It wasn't. I didn't know until much later that they had all been killed.

After hiding out for three days, I was eventually captured by a woodman and taken to a house in a nearby village, guarded by two Hitler youths. An old lady was busy in the kitchen. She ordered the youths out of the kitchen and put her finger to her lips. She went to the

Laurie Woolliscroft outside his parish church at Cannock.

Cannock, Staffordshire.

stove, took out a bowl of soup and shoved it in my hand. She pointed to a photograph on the wall and I understood that this was of her son, who was a prisoner somewhere in England. Then she held the door whilst I finished the soup.

When I returned to England, I wanted to repay in some way the old lady's action. I went to the commandant of the nearby prison camp and asked if I could invite two or three of the German prisoners for Christmas dinner. One of the men who came was called Willie Bretsner, who has since become one of my closest friends. After the war he went back to Germany. He was very poor, and we used to send him clothing and food parcels. I discovered, only about two years ago, on a visit to his home, that he has kept some of that clothing almost as a shrine, to remember how we helped him when he was in dire straits.

All this happened because of one bowl of soup. You could say that if the friendship between Willie and myself were multiplied millions of times, war would be even more futile than it is at the present time.

Hills of the North, rejoice;
  River and mountain-spring,
Hark to the advent voice;
  Valley and lowland, sing;
Though absent long, your Lord is nigh;
He judgment brings and victory.

Isles of the southern sea,
  Deep in your coral caves
Pent be each warring breeze,
  Lulled be your restless waves:
He comes to reign with boundless sway,
And makes your wastes His great highway.

Lands of the East, awake,
  Soon shall your sons be free;
The sleep of ages break,
  And rise to liberty.
On your far hills, long cold and grey,
Has dawned the everlasting day.

Shores of the utmost West,
  Ye that have waited long,
Unvisited, unblest,
  Break forth to swelling song;
Lift up your hearts, your voices raise,
In hymns of everlasting praise.

Shout, while ye journey home;
  Songs be in every mouth;
Lo, from the North we come,
  From East, and West, and South.
City of God, the bond are free,
We come to live and reign in thee!
C. E. Oakley (1832–1865)

Without the kidney machine in his home, David Williams would not be alive today. With its help he can even pursue his favourite hobby – walking the Derbyshire hills.

At the name of Jesus

It was very frightening at first for me and my wife, but we knew it was something we'd got to learn to live with. If I didn't sit here on this machine, I wouldn't be alive. It's as simple as that. The machine is actually cleaning my blood – a thing which my own kidneys cannot do. They packed up about seven years ago, and since then I've been hooked onto the machine twice a week.

My brother had the same problem. That was quite some years ago, and because there were no machines available, he died. When it happened to me, I didn't really think about dying; I just knew I was ill, knew it was serious, and I was thankful that there was this machine available to keep me alive.

It's changed my life an awful lot. It's deepened my faith in God; perhaps a lot of people would have gone the

David Williams has to be hooked onto his kidney machine twice a week.

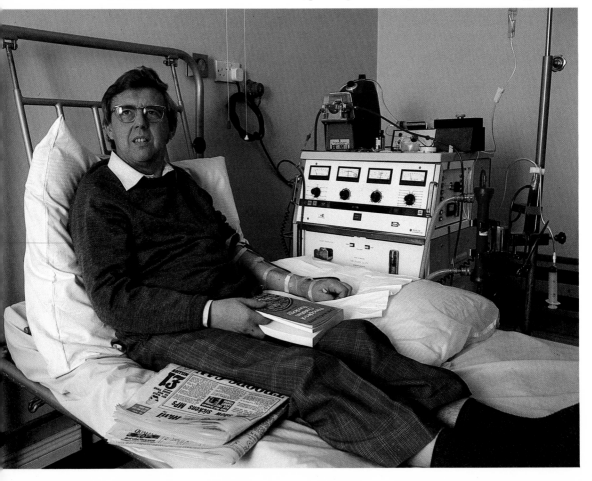

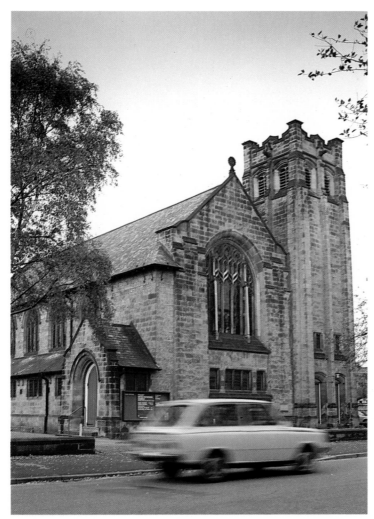

David is training to become an ordained minister in the United Reformed Church. At present he attends this church in Nottingham.

other way. I had a fairly strong faith beforehand, and I think that helped me over the crisis when I was first ill. Then, about four years ago, I became very ill and went into a coma for four days. There was no medical explanation for that coma; I came out of it, I recovered, and within a matter of weeks I was back on my feet again. That set me really thinking and I think it was a sort of turn in my life. I believe that God was working there, helping me to come out of that coma and protecting me.

Then, about three years ago, I felt I had this call to go into the ministry. It was so strong I had to do something about it. I felt that the experiences of illness I had gone through would be a great help in this work. So I have just started training and, at the end of the course, I will be an ordained minister in the United Reformed Church.

At the name of Jesus
Every knee shall bow,
Every tongue confess him
King of Glory now:
'Tis the Father's pleasure
We should call him Lord,
Who from the beginning
Was the mighty Word.

Humbled for a season,
To receive a name
From the lips of sinners
Unto whom he came,
Faithfully he bore it
Spotless to the last,
Brought it back victorious,
When from death he passed.

Name him, brothers, name him,
With love strong as death,
But with awe and wonder
And with bated breath:
He is God the Saviour,
He is Christ the Lord,
Ever to be worshipped,
Trusted, and adored.

In your hearts enthrone him;
There let him subdue
All that is not holy,
All that is not true;
Crown him as your Captain
In temptation's hour;
Let his will enfold you
In its light and power.

Brothers, this Lord Jesus
Shall return again,
With his Father's glory,
With his angel train;
For all wreaths of empire
Meet upon his brow,
And our hearts confess him
King of Glory now.
Caroline M. Noel (1817–77)

I cannot tell

Since appearing on Songs of Praise, Dorothy Gell, a mother of two children, has died of the cancer she faced so courageously.

When I came out of the doctor's surgery, I had a sense of feeling numb and recognising something dramatic had happened in my life. I think I was probably, to a certain extent, in shock. I came home and shared it with my husband, and we went forward from there. We decided that our first step was going to be to commit ourselves and our children into Christ's hands, before we went ahead with hospital treatment or anything. So we did that; we went, as a family, to a service of laying on of hands.

I don't think at any time I felt bitter, nor my husband either – lots of Christians have difficulties, many have harder difficulties than I have had. You can be frightened of dying, you can be frightened of anything, but my prayer has helped enormously. Sometimes, if I've got a pain, I sort of gulp and say: Oh dear, I've got something else to go through. But that's only temporary; I concentrate on the Lord, and go forward with him.

All my family know that I have cancer. Needless to say, with a young family, they don't understand it, but

Farmland near Hereford, where Dorothy Gell lived.

as far as I'm concerned, the children are wonderful; sometimes if I haven't been feeling a hundred per cent – and cancer sufferers very often don't want to get going, they want to sort of curl up if they can – the thought of the children has helped me. I've been given a responsibility and I'm going to try and do my best. I know that our Lord will take care of them.

The hymn that I've chosen really has two aspects: the first is that things can't be fully explained, but the second is that we can have confidence in Jesus Christ, not only for this life, but also for the next. That's my philosophy and that's how I live.

I cannot tell why he, whom angels worship,
   Should set his love upon the sons of men,
Or why, as Shepherd, he should seek the wanderers,
   To bring them back, they know not how or when.
But this I know, that he was born of Mary
   When Bethlehem's manager was his only home,
And that he lived at Nazareth and laboured,
   And so the Saviour, Saviour of the world, is come.

I cannot tell how silently he suffered,
   As with his peace he graced this place of tears,
Or how his heart upon the cross was broken,
   The crown of pain to three and thirty years.
But this I know, he heals the broken-hearted,
   And stays our sin and calms our lurking fear,
And lifts the burden from the heavy laden,
   For yet the Saviour, Saviour of the world, is here.

I cannot tell how he will win the nations,
   How he will claim his earthly heritage,
How satisfy the needs and aspirations
   Of east and west, of sinner and of sage.
But this I know, all flesh shall see his glory,
   And he shall reap the harvest he has sown,
And some glad day his sun shall shine in splendour
   When he the Saviour, Saviour of the world, is known.

I cannot tell how all the lands shall worship,
   When at his bidding every storm is stilled,
Or who can say how great the jubilation,
   When all the hearts of men with love are filled.
But this I know, the skies will thrill with rapture,
   And myriad myriad human voices sing,
And earth to heaven, and heaven to earth, will answer:
   'At last the Saviour, Saviour of the world, is King!'
William Young Fullerton (1857–1932)

The Music

Hymns and their background

Music is one of the most important aspects of worship for many people. It is often a deeply felt part of spirituality, since it calls forth hidden emotions and feelings, and it also helps us to express delight and enthusiasm. Whether we are being uplifted by hearing the music, or enjoying taking part, it helps us to express our religious feelings in ways that words alone cannot do.

In *Songs of Praise* it is the delight of joining in which is emphasised, not only by all the people in the church, but also by all those who sing along with the hymns and songs at home. Even if we are ill or housebound, the programme gives us an opportunity to offer our praises to God together – and its enthusiasm is infectious!

Hymns are traditionally the people's music of the church, originating as the part of worship which was *not* the exclusive territory of the clergy. They have been sung in imitation, line by line, by people who could not read ('lining out'), and they have been passed down the generations by repeated singing and learning (oral tradition). They have largely remained the property of the people as their part in church worship, in great public occasions, and even in the football stands.

Hymns link us with the early Christians: St Paul tells us to 'speak to one another in psalms, hymns and spiritual songs; sing and make music in your hearts to the Lord' (Ephesians 5:19). But it is the ancient psalms, those timeless outpourings of joy and suffering, which led to the growth of the kind of hymns we know and love.

The Reformation in the sixteenth century forced Christianity to communicate better by translating the Bible and the Prayer Book into the vernacular, which made them more generally accessible; and it is from this period that the metrical psalms – psalms versified so that they could be sung to simple tunes – began our modern hymnody.

The most famous hymn from that time is 'All People That On Earth Do Dwell' – and its tune is still called 'The Old Hundredth' because the hymn is a metrical version of Psalm 100 from that first 'old' metrical psalter.

Michael Armitage is Music Adviser to Songs of Praise.

Choosing the hymns

Ask people to choose their favourite hymns, and you would expect the list to be endless. But in fact there seem to be only a handful which are everyone's favourites. They will almost certainly include 'The Lord's my Shepherd', 'Abide with me', 'When I survey the wondrous cross' and 'Guide me, O thou great Redeemer'.

Some, if not all, of these appear in our choice lists every week. This could mean *Songs of Praise* ending up with the same six hymns every week!

Luckily everyone is asked to choose three hymns, which broadens the scope; and some people will have novel choices or special reasons which add variety. In this way we are able to include lesser known hymns and new songs, like 'Make me a channel of your peace' and Sydney Carter's 'Lord of the Dance', which are now firm favourites. Other suggestions are made by the ecumenical steering committees of local church leaders who organise those taking part.

The church's main festivals, like Christmas or even saints' days, have also been an inspiration for hymns, and this also influences the hymns chosen for a particular programme.

The first and last hymns in each programme must be exactly right to welcome us to the programme and to sing us out again. And they have to be long enough to let us look around the church at the beginning and to say farewell to the people we have met at the end. Since they may also have to be relevant to the season of the church's year, they have to be chosen with great care. If it is the first Sunday in Advent, for instance, two of the best choices wuld be 'O come, O come Emmanuel' and 'Lo, he comes with clouds descending'.

The choir assembles for rehearsals at Carisbrooke Castle, Isle of Wight.

A young trombonist accompanies the singing at Croydon Parish Church.

A section of the choir at Croydon Parish Church.

If there is a famous local hymnwriter or composer then the second hymn may well reflect this; or it may feature a special local group, like a children's choir, if they are involved in local worship.

The remaining five hymns are chosen by the individual Christians interviewed, and the programme is then balanced by the selection of tunes and the musical arrangements made. Although most people mention the words of their hymns, the tunes have often played an important part in influencing their choice, and so we have to pay special attention to the best way to perform them.

Musical resources

Each area *Songs of Praise* visits has its local traditions and resources for music making in its worship. The organ is the most common, but if we are in Cornwall there is a great tradition of unaccompanied choral singing, and in the North of England brass bands are often used. Many Roman Catholic churches were not built with organs, and so, after Vatican II, they have increasingly used instruments in the folk tradition. Inner city pentecostal churches often use electric groups to accompany their singing.

We believe that the breadth of local music making in church worship should be reflected in *Songs of Praise*, and so we try to include some of these elements, or others similar, each week.

Much depends on the conductor at this stage, and, when he has been chosen, he will discuss with the Producer and the Music Adviser which of the local musical resources it would be best to use. If there's an orchestra, are orchestrations already available, or can they be done quickly? Which of the folk groups should be used? Will we offend one group if we choose another? Could they play together? Will there be a children's item – do they want to play instruments or just sing? Which hymns would be better for organ alone? Will there be an organ tuner standing by if our hot lights affect the pitch? Shall we have descants? Will they be sung or instrumental?

All of this has to be worked out quickly, so that the choirs, the instrumentalists and the organist all know what will be expected of them. Finally the Producer can work out the best way to capture the right atmosphere for the television screen.

There is no substitute for good singing, whatever resources are available. So, after the hymns are chosen, the hard work begins, with taxing choir practices for the several hundreds of local singers who will form the core of the singing congregation: 'Tenors – not so loud.' 'Altos, you're flat! Keep your eyes on the Conductor!' At this stage the conductors usually realise what a mammoth task they have taken on! But it is also at this stage that the BBC back-up can be of the greatest help, since the hymn book will be provided, and the Music Adviser will be on hand to support the conductor.

The Hymn Book

The most useful resource is the Hymn Book which is prepared and printed by the BBC. For copyright reasons it has to be destroyed after use, but it will bear the fruit of many hours of careful work.

Often the children are asked to sing by themselves.

The church buildings used for Songs of Praise must be large enough to allow the cameras room to manoeuvre.

Because of the nature of hymns, having been handed on through generations, people tend to know different versions of words and tunes. Consequently we have a large library of hymn books and song collections, to ensure that we get the right version. We search for the most authentic versions of (a) the tunes and (b) the words.

The tunes
Because tunes have been sung and communicated by ear for many years, changes tend to creep in. 'When I survey the wondrous cross' (Rockingham) began life as a popular song, and was adapted as a hymn by Edward Miller in 1790. (Many hymns have begun life in this way – 'Stand up, stand up for Jesus' (Morning Light) began as a drawing-room ballad called 'Hark, the lark is singing!') In the version familiar to us, Rockingham has a G sharp in the tune near the end of the line 'My richest

gain I count but loss'; but Samuel Webbe, who harmonised it beautifully in his 1808 *Collection of Psalm Tunes,* actually wrote a G flat in the melody line, which was probably more authentic. The *Songs of Praise* team tried this out at one church, but as everyone was used to the 'wrong' version, we had to give it up!

In 'Guide me, O thou great Redeemer' (or Jehovah!) the tune *Cwm Rhondda* usually lets us belt out high D's when we sing 'Feed me now and evermore'. But John Hughes' tune originally swept down the scale and up to the top again – so we ask congregations to sing that version instead: not only is it more authentic, it also saves their voices!

Revd Michael Armitage passes on some musical tips to his choir.

Praying or planning? A BBC cameraman prepares to film Songs of Praise.

The words
The texts of hymns have usually been subjected to a great deal of editing through the years, and some recent hymn books have even tried to eliminate the worst

obscurities of ancient language and bad translations; all of which now makes it difficult to settle for any one version of the words of some hymns. We try to discover the intentions of the original author, and then make a decision to print either the first or an edited version of the words.

Recording the music

There will be several rehearsals for the main group of singers, and sectional rehearsals for orchestras, bands, groups and children. During these rehearsals any problems with arrangements must be solved, and the Producer makes notes of timings and the details of who does what in each of the hymns.

At last, when everything is thoroughly rehearsed and ready, everyone comes together for the two main sessions with the TV cameras and sound equipment, as the climax of months of hard and detailed work.

Although we usually sing our *Songs of Praise* in a church building, it can never be like a normal church service. There are many distractions because of the placing of the bright lights, the moving of cameras and the positioning of microphones and other equipment. And the place will be full – with hundreds of people from different churches and chapels – sometimes for the first time. Everyone will have to put more effort into their singing and praising God than they ever have before. Perhaps our normal services would gain a great deal if everyone put as much energy into them as well!

The great thing is that putting your heart and soul into singing with so many others is such a marvellously enjoyable experience it brings out qualities people never suspected they had. Many who have taken part in *Songs of Praise* programmes tell us how much they have got out of the occasion, and how spiritually uplifting it has been, not only to join in the singing, but also to know that it will be a help to millions who will be part of it, enjoying it in their own homes.

At a time when we are very aware of our various divisions and the church is said to be failing, it is wonderful to be part of an important religious musical experience which binds people together, and cuts across our petty differences, as we share the excitement of singing our praises to God.

'Bless the Lord all people on earth:
Sing his praise and exalt him for ever.
Let everything that has breath praise the Lord.
O praise the Lord.'

Michael Armitage

If there are unusual musical resources available, the Music Adviser will try to utilise them.

Hymns from the Psalms

Concern for his own sons on the streets of Brixton led Astell Parkinson first to start a drop-in club in his own backyard, and then to leave his job as a bus driver to go into youth work full-time.

The Lord's my Shepherd

Before he became a full-time youth-worker, Astell worked on the London buses.

At that time there wasn't much places around for kids to go in the evenings, so I changed my yard into a kind of dropping-in point for them to play dominoes, weight-lifting, what-have-you. Before long we were catering for a lot of kids in there – it was a place they could come to and make themselves at home.

And now it's the same at St. Matthew's. The work we carry on is simple; we play games, and they can wander in off the street, and are welcome to join in whatever activity is going on. For many it's a kind of sanctuary; they come in and know that nobody's going to interfere

with them. And for those few hours they're here, they feel safe.

People have a very bad image of black kids in Brixton, but that is far different from what is really happening. There are a great number of young people in Brixton, black and white, who have done well, very well. There are people who think that youngsters are trouble-makers, but I think it's fear on both sides – the kids are afraid to trespass onto the territory of those who are afraid of them, and they're afraid to trespass onto the kids'.

So a place like St. Matthew's is a place where they can get rid of such fears. At the same time, we can build up a relationship between those two groups, old and young, because our building is not only a youth club, it's used for other groups as well, and often the young people are coming in while the older ones are going out.

I think I am a Christian in my belief; maybe not a

Brixton, South London.

true, practising Christian, but I have Christian belief. If I started preaching Christianity to these kids, they'd throw me out. That's the honest truth. We try to tell them: 'Look, the building you are in used to be a church – the point is, be respectable. If you want to swear, find a corner and swear your head off, as long as you don't offend anybody else.' That's the only principle we force on them.

The hymn I chose, 'The Lord's my Shepherd', is a song I knew ever since I was a child. When I travelled to this country, I requested that hymn to be sung and, when I arrived, I bought the record of it. If I sit down and listen to that hymn, or even hum it, I feel more relaxed. I feel that there is somebody up there, around me, or somewhere, who I can call to.

Astell Parkinson runs a youth club at St Matthews, Brixton.

The Lord's my Shepherd, I'll not want;
*   He makes me down to lie*
In pastures green; he leadeth me
*   The quiet waters by.*

My soul he doth restore again,
*   And me to walk doth make*
Within the paths of righteousness,
*   E'en for his own name's sake.*

Yea, though I walk in death's dark vale,
*   Yet will I fear no ill;*
For thou art with me, and thy rod
*   And staff me comfort still.*

My table thou hast furnishèd
*   In presence of my foes;*
My head thou dost with oil anoint
*   And my cup overflows.*

Goodness and mercy all my life
*   Shall surely follow me;*
And in God's house for evermore
*   My dwelling-place shall be.*

Scottish Psalter (1650). Based on Psalm 23

The God of Love

Kidnapped by Protestant extremists, Father Hugh Murphy discovered a lot of things – about himself, about prayer, and about the terrible divisions of Northern Ireland.

Hugh Murphy, tell us about the day you were kidnapped.
Oh, why do you want to bring that old thing up? Well, I was lured out of my house early one summer morning on the plea that someone needed me, and, when I opened the front door, there was a gun pointed at me. They whipped me away, blindfolded me, tied my hands behind my back and kept me that way all day. I was sure I was going to die. I was really a hostage for a policeman who had been injured the day before; those fellows who kidnapped me somehow thought that through me, or my church, the men of violence might be brought to see sense.

I learned a lot of things that day. One of them was the power of prayer. I prayed for calmness, and I got it. I

Father Murphy is a parish priest in Coleraine, County Londonderry, Northern Ireland.

think nearly all Northern Ireland were praying for me, Protestant and Catholic, both in church and at home. But I was very lucky to survive.

What has been the lasting effect of that experience?
The first effect is fear; you know, when the stairs squeak at night now, I see them coming for me again. Or if I see a car following me or following my car around, I begin to wonder. I'm afraid of so many things now, especially of opening the door on a Sunday morning.

But more than that, I feel very sad for the men who kidnapped me, and I feel, more than ever, a greater need to build bridges across our community in Northern Ireland.

How real is that gap?
Incredible. And, in a sad way, sort of amusing. You see,

Father Murphy meets some of his young parishioners in the street.

Catholics read one morning paper, Protestants another; Catholics go to one village for their summer holidays, Protestants to another. They even say, believe it or not, that there is a Catholic way of doing the Glens of Antrim, where you go from one Catholic village to another, and there's a Protestant way, where you never see a Catholic village!

And yet we all have so much in common. I learned this many years ago, when I was helping to start the Samaritans here; we were working with Protestant clergymen, and I found they hadn't horns, and I hope they found I hadn't any either. Before I die, the one thing I'd love to do would be to find a formula, and I think there is one somewhere, that would unite this sad, warring community. Let us emphasise the things we have in common rather than the things which keep us apart.

Coleraine, County Londonderry.

The God of love my Shepherd is,
And he that doth me feed;
While he is mine and I am his,
What can I want or need?

He leads me to the tender grass,
Where I both feed and rest;
Then to the streams that gently pass:
In both I have the best.

Or if I stray, he doth convert,
And bring my mind in frame;
And all this not for my desert,
But for his holy name.

Yea, in death's shady black abode
Well may I walk, not fear;
For thou art with me, and thy rod
To guide, thy staff to bear.

Surely thy sweet and wondrous love
Shall measure all my days;
And, as it never shall remove,
So neither shall my praise.

George Herbert (1593–1632) Psalm 23

Before he was even tall enough to reach the pedals, Mark Venning was enthralled by organs and organ music. Later he trained as an organist, taught music for a while, and now heads a firm of organ builders.

Jesus shall reign

Mark Venning has permission to play the organ of Durham Cathedral late at night, when nobody's there!

The way we make organs has remained remarkably constant through the years – we do make use of modern materials, but the techniques, basically very accurate wood-work, are just the same as they were a hundred years ago.

The first step in making an organ is to go and see the particular building in which it is going to stand, because all our organs are individually made – there are no two alike. Then we draw up a special design for the appearance of the organ and the particular musical content that is needed. Then comes the wood-work.

Much of the mechanism is made of wood; the pipes are mostly made of metal, and are of various shapes and sizes. The longest pipes we make here are thirty-two feet long (the organ in Durham Cathedral has three of that length), and the shortest are less than one inch.

A very important part of organ building is what we call voicing. This is the process by which the pipes are made to give a good musical sound. It's rather like tuning an orchestra; the voicer has to adjust all the various parts of the pipes in minute detail, to get them to speak correctly, and he does this all over again once the organ is installed in the church.

One of the best things about being an organ builder is the terrific interest that there is in this instrument. I believe the main reason is the unique musical excitement of the pipe organ: nobody has discovered anything like its expressive range and power.

Durham Cathedral organ is a very special one for us, of course; we've looked after it since 1904. I'm very lucky – I'm allowed to go into the cathedral late at night and play the organ when nobody's there. It's a magical experience to be in the cathedral when it is totally deserted and dark.

I've chosen the hymn 'Jesus shall reign' because the tune is by a former organist of Durham Cathedral.

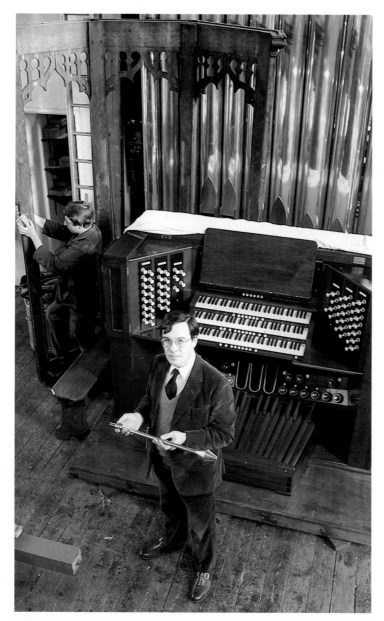

Durham Cathedral.

Mark now heads up a leading firm of organ builders in Durham, but still enjoys playing the organ whenever he can.

Jesus shall reign where'er the sun
Doth his successive journeys run;
His kingdom stretch from shore to shore,
Till moons shall wax and wane no more.

People and realms of every tongue
Dwell on his love with sweetest song,
And infant voices shall proclaim
Their early blessings on his name.

Blessings abound where'er he reigns;
The prisoner leaps to lose his chains;
The weary find eternal rest,
And all the sons of want are blest.

Let every creature rise and bring
Peculiar honours to our King;
Angels descend with songs again,
And earth repeat the long amen.

Isaac Watts (1674–1748) Psalm 72

One of the many men who lost their eyesight during World War II, Bill Kay now leads a busy and contented life in a home for the war-blinded.

O God, our help in ages past

Bill Kay lost his sight as a result of serious malnutrition while serving in India and Burma during the war.

Bill Kay now lives at the War Blinded Institute at Linburn, Midlothian. This picture of the nearby countryside includes the famous Forth Bridge.

I was in the 129 Field Regiment. We went first to India and then Burma. We were attached to a very famous Indian division, and we supported them in a lot of big actions. Well, I became very ill with dysentery and malaria. We were in action most of the time, things were pretty grim and, of course, the food was very poor. From then on it seemed to affect my sight. The doctors later said it was actually a form of malnutrition which, in some cases, leads to loss of sight.

While we were in action, every now and then, the Padre, who was a great lad, would turn up from nowhere and, within minutes he was organising a service – under some trees, in a shack or even once, I remember, in a battered old rice mill. He boosted the morale, you know; nobody, not even the toughest soldier, will deny that, when things got really tough, they said a prayer.

But we always thought we were going to win; there was no question of giving up the ghost or throwing in the towel. Even in the worst of the grim struggles, when you tucked yourself into your mosquito net at night, it was amazing how many times the words of the hymn that I've chosen, 'Oh God, our help in ages past', came back to you when you needed help.

There was a time when we despaired of ever seeing Scotland again, but eventually we pushed on and we made it, and most of us got home. I was very distressed

at first, because I obviously couldn't go back to my old job in the Water Department; so I was brought here very confused, but I soon settled down. It's a great place; I've got wonderful friends here and we get every possible advice and assistance. I work in the plastics shop and we make a great variety of things from wallets and door-stops to toy soldiers and envelopes. I enjoy it.

I love walking here; it's so peaceful and quiet and away from all the traffic. There are white rails all around the estate, so that even a totally blind chap can have a good walk, holding the rail, right round the grounds and back to his house, or the workshops, or wherever he wants to go.

I suppose in the end you get accustomed to being blind. One of our greatest comedians here is totally blind. There's a terrific sense of fun here – we're probably a happier lot in this place than you'd get anywhere else!

At the War Blinded Institute, Bill is able to work in the plastics shop, and read braille books.

O God, our help in ages past,
  Our hope for years to come,
Our shelter from the stormy blast,
  And our eternal home;

Beneath the shadow of thy throne
  Thy saints have dwelt secure;
Sufficient is thine arm alone,
  And our defence is sure.

Before the hills in order stood,
  Or earth received her frame,
From everlasting thou art God,
  To endless years the same.

A thousand ages in thy sight
  Are like an evening gone;
Short as the watch that ends the night
  Before the rising sun.

Time, like an ever-rolling stream,
  Bears all its sons away;
They fly forgotten, as a dream
  Dies at the opening day.

O God, our help in ages past,
  Our hope for years to come,
Be thou our guard while troubles last,
  And our eternal home.

Isaac Watts (1674–1748) Based on Psalm 90

Cardinal Basil Hume, Archbishop of Westminster, sees the singing of hymns together as one important part in the slow process of bringing Christians of all persuasions into unity with each other.

The Old Hundredth

If I happen to be near a television set on a Sunday, and it's only in my recent past or on my holidays that that's been possible, I watch *Songs of Praise*. I've always believed it to be good because it brings together Christians from different churches to pray together and sing hymns together.

The most important thing that man can do is worship God, and one of the nicest and best ways of worshipping God is to sing his praises – to use what is best in music and in speech in order to try and convey what lies deepest in us.

And I really do believe that another of the most important things that we can do is to pray together. It's all very well for people like bishops to talk about unity, but what really matters in the end is what happens locally in the parish, and I'm very anxious that people in parishes should get together to pray.

It's very important to me personally that Christians of different denominations should come together. One of the reasons is that my own family was mixed – part Catholic and part non-Catholic – and, from very earliest childhood, I saw the sheer goodness of the non-Catholic members of my family. It was the Lord's wish that we should be one, and we need no other reason than that.

Westminster Cathedral, London.

Also, I think Christianity has been so much part of our culture, part of our English heritage, that to think that that heritage is divided is painful too.

The hymn that I would like to select is what they call The Old Hundredth, 'All people that on earth do dwell'. I say that because, about a decade ago, when I was in Rome for the canonisation of the forty martyrs, that was the hymn we sang as we entered into the basilica of St Peter's. On that day St Peter's had become an English parish church. It was an astonishingly moving moment. It was for that reason that I asked that it should be sung when I entered Westminster Cathedral on the day that I was ordained a bishop. So it holds all kinds of memories.

All people that on earth do dwell,
Sing to the Lord with cheerful voice;
Him serve with fear, his praise forth tell,
Come ye before him, and rejoice.

The Lord, ye know, is God indeed;
Without our aid he did us make;
We are his folk, he doth us feed,
And for his sheep he doth us take.

O enter then his gates with praise,
Approach with joy his courts unto;
Praise, laud, and bless his name always,
For it is seemly so to do.

For why? the Lord our God is good;
His mercy is for ever sure;
His truth at all times firmly stood,
And shall from age to age endure.

To Father, Son, and Holy Ghost,
The God whom heaven and earth adore,
From men and from the angel-host
Be praise and glory evermore.

W. Kethe (d. 1594) Based on Psalm 100

The River Thames near West-minster.

Dorothy Mindham has two creative hobbies: painting and nature conservation. Here she describes how her interest in painting began, when her life was particularly difficult.

O worship the King

Dorothy Mindham chose a hymn that expresses her love for the countryside.

I was housebound with two elderly parents to care for. It had become necessary to give up my part-time job and almost all activities outside the home, because they could no longer look after themselves, or be left alone in safety. I know it's a common enough experience, but, at the best of times, it's never easy. Anyone in the same situation will know the bad days and nights, when perhaps it seems that things can't get any worse.

But, looking back, I can see that good came out of it; I learnt the value of real friendship from people who simply kept in touch. I learnt more about myself, and I began to understand a little better what my faith meant to me. At that time, when one was sometimes too tired to think straight, it wasn't an intellectual thing at all, it was a strength, an underpinning, and when I let it be, it was a quietness. Although I didn't see it at the time, as one sort of life was coming to an end, another one was opening up.

I bought myself some paints. I'd always thought I should like to paint, and now I felt I needed to. I think it was a way of coming to terms with my situation. A good friend gave me a lesson or two, I read all I could, and the rest was trial and error! It was challenging, exasperating sometimes, and totally absorbing. Just what I needed at that time.

And when I came through the difficult times, these two wonderful things remained, that I was able to develop and bring together – my love of the countryside and my enjoyment in painting it.

The hymn I've chosen is a song of delight in the things of creation, and of wonder and awe at God, the creative spirit at the heart of the universe and all our experience. This appeals to me as a painter because of my love of the countryside, particularly Norfolk with its beautiful wide-open skies and lovely light.

O worship the King all glorious above;
O gratefully sing his power and his love;
Our Shield and Defender, the Ancient of Days,
Pavilioned in splendour and girded with praise.

O tell of his might, O sing of his grace,
Whose robe is the light, whose canopy space;
His chariots of wrath the deep thunder clouds form,
And dark is his path on the wings of the storm.

The earth with its store of wonders untold,
Almighty, thy power hath founded of old;
Hath stablished it fast by a changeless decree,
And round it hath cast, like a mantle, the sea.

Thy bountiful care what tongue can recite?
It breathes in the air, it shines in the light;
It streams from the hills, it descends to the plain,
And sweetly distils in the dew and the rain.

Frail children of dust and feeble as frail,
In thee do we trust, nor find thee to fail;
Thy mercies how tender, how firm to the end!
Our Maker, Defender, Redeemer, and Friend.

O measureless Might, ineffable Love,
While angels delight to hymn thee above,
Thy ransomed creation, though feeble their lays,
With true adoration shall sing to thy praise.

Robert Grant (1779–1838) Based on Psalm 104

Bishop's Bridge, Norwich; a
favourite spot for local artists.

Farming the land that his father and grandfather did before him, Alastair MacCallum cares for 1,900 sheep spread over 4,000 acres of Scottish hillside.

I to the hills will lift mine eyes

Alastair MacCallum has a sheep farm in the Scottish hills near Fort William, Inverness.

Working in the hills can be a very hard life, with weather conditions to contend with – wind and rain, and snowstorms in the winter time. It can be quite frightening at times, if there's a high wind blowing.

Each man is responsible for his own sheep and has to see that they are in safety at the time of a storm coming. Sheep themselves are very good weather-judges; they often come down by themselves. But there are always a few that stay up in some little ravine or stuck behind a forestry block, and you have to be very careful that they are not covered by snow-drifts up there. If there are

sheep missing and there's heavy snow drifting, you have to go along and poke in the burns – you go to whatever lengths you can to find them. That is your job as a shepherd.

I live very near to nature and I appreciate the beauty of the hills, but in spite of that I sometimes have attacks

As a shepherd, Alastair MacCallum is responsible for some 1,900 sheep, making sure they are safe in bad weather.

of depression. I've had many kinds of treatment for it, and swallowed hundreds of pills; they certainly help, but nobody can tell me what causes the depression.

You are very apt to blame yourself; everything looks very black and you lose your confidence completely. Some people may say to you: 'Just snap out of it', but they don't know what they're talking about; you can't do that. It's quite impossible. And at those times, I feel that my faith means an awful lot to me: God is always near me. I can feel his presence very real.

I have chosen the Scottish psalm, 'I to the hills'. This psalm means a lot to me in my work, living in the hills and seeing God's creation. In it I find many promises which God has fulfilled. It is very dear to me.

Alastair MacCallum sometimes suffers from black depression; it is at such times that his faith means much to him.

I to the hills will lift mine eyes.
From whence doth come mine aid?
My safety cometh from the Lord,
Who heaven and earth hath made.

Thy foot he'll not let slide, nor will
*   He slumber that thee keeps.*
Behold, he that keeps Israel,
*   He slumbers not, nor sleeps.*

The Lord shall keep thy soul; he shall
*   Preserve thee from all ill.*
Henceforth thy going out and in
*   God keep for ever will.*

The Lord thee keeps, the Lord thy shade
*   On thy right hand doth stay;*
The moon by night thee shall not smite,
*   Nor yet the sun by day.*

To Father, Son, and Holy Ghost,
*   The God whom we adore,*
Be glory, as it was, and is,
*   And shall be evermore.*

Based on Psalm 121

Pilgrimage

With thirteen years as an officer in the infantry and a Military Cross to his credit, Tom Hiney now has a rather different role in the army – working as a padre.

Who would true valour see

Revd Tom Hiney sees his role as that of bringing soldiers and their families closer to God.

I find it an exhilarating job. It's impossible to know quite how one succeeds – there's no visible end product – but it is exhilarating. It does, however, require complete and utter belief. There is no point in moralising alone; morality without faith is very sterile and the soldiers would rightly regard it as boring. It's got to be infused by a living faith, and, if one's lucky enough to have one, one just attempts to bring God into the lives of other people – with varying degrees of success.

I've never had any problem about being first a Christian and now a padre in the army. I regard the commandment 'Thou shalt not kill' as what it says in the original: 'Thou shalt not commit murder'. It's nothing to do with killing in self-defence.

If we felt it was immoral even to defend our own country, we shouldn't be in the army. We know for certain that some soldiers are deeply distressed if they kill somebody, and I would do my best to tell them that they're perfectly at ease with their own God, if they believe in God. Whilst we prepare soliders for danger, we would certainly never encourage them to be over-joyful about winning when it has involved killing people.

I regard the role of padre as bringing soldiers and their families nearer to God, and bringing God nearer to the soldiers. A padre is in the system yet out of it; we identify by wearing uniform, rank and so forth, but we have free access into the guardrooms and the hospitals. And of course, in the barracks and the headquarters where we operate we are made welcome wherever we go.

One of the jobs of a padre is to identify himself with soldiers on exercises, which take up something like one third of their time, and to take services there and then. There is no compulsion on soldiers in barracks to attend services, except on Remembrance Sunday; but in the field services are compulsory. They only last fifteen to twenty minutes, and the soldiers like it; very, very few object. I accept completely that some people aren't sure whether they believe in God or not, but, in an organisation where the soldiers are likely to be under fire, or in danger, or travelling about, they are more ready to think deeply about the truths of life.

The School of Infantry, Warminster, Wiltshire.

Who would true valour see,
Let him come hither;
One here will constant be,
Come wind, come weather.
There's no discouragement
Shall make him once relent
His first avowed intent
To be a pilgrim.

Whoso beset him round
With dismal stories,
Do but themselves confound;
His strength the more is.
No lion can him fright,
He'll with a giant fight,
But he will have a right
To be a pilgrim.

Hobgoblin nor foul fiend
Can daunt his spirit:
He knows he at the end
Shall life inherit.
Then fancies fly away,
He'll fear not what men say,
He'll labour night and day
To be a pilgrim.

John Bunyan (1628–88)

Until Argentina invaded the Falklands, sunken ships off the islands were a matter of academic study for John Smith. Then it became a tragic reality.

Guide me, O thou great Redeemer

John Smith lived through the difficult days of the Falklands War in 1982; he believes his faith was strengthened during that time.

I first came to the Falklands in 1957 as part of the British Antarctic Survey. I did two and a half years with the survey, and during that time visited Stanley a number of times and came to like the place. It's completely unspoiled and untouched, probably just as God left it after he finished making it; I reckon that when he was building the rest of the world, he shoved all the bits and off-cuts under a bench and, at the end of the day, he said, well all right, these bits are the Falklands! Thus we've got this lovely conglomeration of mountains, slopes, plains, green grass, yellow grass. It's a wonderful place to bring up children – by the time ours were twelve, they were able to drive a land-rover, shoot a goose, catch a trout or change a wheel – all the sensible things in life.

When I came here, it was a completely open field as regards the maritime history of the Falklands, and I've been working on that ever since. It's especially important because this was the last resting place of many of the Cape Horn era ships. I've plotted the positions of some 200 sailing ships wrecked in and around the Falklands since 1833.

The sinking of any ship and the loss of sailors is a sad occasion, no matter whose side they are on, but it's a bit too much on your own door-step. The *Sir Tristram* was a tragic sight, towed in, still smoking, three or four weeks after being bombed. And now she's a constant reminder of what war is all about.

It's very difficult when you sit down and try to analyse it. Obviously we want to retain our way of life, our country, our freedom. But, at the same time, when you see dead people lying about on places where you would normally have taken the dog for a walk, where the children would have gone out to play, it gives you a period of doubt, you don't quite know which way to go. Obviously, if those people were allowed, they would kill you, so you've got to stand up and kill them, but it does make you see how useless and stupid the whole thing is.

I think our faith as Catholics was reinforced during the occupation. I'm sure everyone in Stanley, whether they had faith or not, offered up prayers on the night of

Many ships were destroyed or seriously damaged during the bitter conflict in the Falklands.

A strong British military presence has now been established in the Falklands.

the invasion, and the faith kept us going. It was very sad in our little church at St Mary's because many of the Argentines, mostly very young, would come in and sit down for an hour or so to regain their sanity. They were totally bewildered, some didn't know where they were – thought they were in Chile – some of them prayed, some just sat and shook.

If you asked anyone in the Task Force who landed at San Carlos and then yomped all the seventy miles to Stanley, I'm sure they'd agree it is a great and barren land, as in the hymn I have chosen; 'Guide me, O thou great Redeemer'. I'm sure, too, that they, as we, asked for guidance and obviously got it.

> *Guide me, O thou great Redeemer,*
>   *Pilgrim through this barren land;*
> *I am weak, but thou art mighty;*
>   *Hold me with thy powerful hand:*
>   *Bread of heaven,*
> *Feed me now and evermore.*
>
> *Open now the crystal fountain*
>   *Whence the healing stream doth flow;*
> *Let the fiery cloudy pillar*
>   *Lead me all my journey through:*
>   *Strong deliverer,*
> *Be thou still my strength and shield.*
>
> *When I tread the verge of Jordan,*
>   *Bid my anxious fears subside;*
> *Death of death, and hell's destruction,*
>   *Land me safe on Canaan's side:*
>   *Songs and praises*
> *I will ever give to thee.*

W. Williams (1717–91) Tr. P. and W. Williams

Lead us, heavenly Father, lead us

When the Argentines invaded the Falklands, Willy Bowles suddenly found himself spokesman and interpreter for 119 islanders locked in a church hall under armed guard.

On the night of the 1st April, the Governor announced over the radio that an invasion was imminent before dawn. My wife's sister rang from Goose Green asking me to take her son back out there as soon as possible. We decided to go under cover of darkness, and we rounded Sapper's Hill at about half-past one in the morning, just as the lights and signals from the Argentines were coming up from Mullet Creek.

We eventually arrived about quarter-to-seven in the morning, and the people of Goose Green persuaded us to stay on there, partly for safety reasons, and partly because I do speak a little bit of Spanish, and they thought it was inevitable that the Argentines would eventually reach Darwin.

Willy Bowles was one of the few people in Goose Green who could speak a little Spanish; he was invaluable as an interpreter with the Argentines.

Several war cemeteries have now been created on the Falkland Islands.

This happened, of course, on 4th April. Their commandos came in by helicopter, crept around the gorse bushes, and entered the settlement. Apart from confiscating the CB radios, any transmitters, and any weapons like rifles that anybody had, they let life continue more or less as normal throughout April.

But on 1st May, when the first Harrier strikes came in, an aircraft came straight down the gorse line and took out a few Argentine positions there, a tentful of aero-engineers and a couple of aircraft. This annoyed the Argentine Airforce something terrific, and they rounded us all up at half-past-seven in the morning. Some people hadn't had their breakfast, and some children were still in bed; but word got round that everybody had to come to the church hall for a meeting we were told would last fifteen minutes. It lasted nearer twenty-eight days.

The first day, they left us there until eight o'clock at night before we could even get any food. After a long harangue with the guards on the door, they eventually let the storekeeper go and get some food for us.

There we remained for various numbers of days; some people got out before others. It wasn't easy with 119 people in the hall; but depression never reigned for very long. They were terrific, especially the children; and we had three people over eighty years old, who were an example to all of us. We never lost hope; we knew the Task Force was on its way, and I think everybody prayed secretly to themselves that we'd remain safe, and that did a terrific amount of good.

Because of my Spanish, I was the one elected to do the talking, but I felt they were all helping me by their prayers through God. I never felt afraid; every time the Argentines came to the door and shouted for me, I always felt I'd come back (though sometimes my wife had her doubts I think).

On one occasion during those dark days, I think it was a Sunday night, we asked the Argentines if they could send their padre along to have a sort of formal service with us and say some prayers. They agreed, and our people were so pleased with him. He was a very nice chap indeed, not interested in the war at all. Much later, when the paras came in and the Argentinians surrendered, I went over and spoke to him again: 'Well father,' I said, 'I think a lot of people's prayers have been answered today.' He said: 'Yes, including mine.'

The special Songs of Praise from the Falkland Islands included music from military bandsmen, and a choir of 400 servicemen on a ship in Port Stanley.

Lead us, heavenly Father, lead us
O'er the world's tempestuous sea;
Guard us, guide us, keep us, feed us,
For we have no help but thee;
Yet possessing every blessing
If our God our Father be.

Saviour, breathe forgiveness o'er us;
All our weakness thou dost know,
Thou didst tread this earth before us,
Thou didst feel its keenest woe;
Lone and dreary, faint and weary,
Through the desert thou didst go.

Spirit of our God, descending,
Fill our hearts with heavenly joy,
Love with every passion blending,
Pleasure that can never cloy:
Thus provided, pardoned, guided,
Nothing can our peace destroy.

James Edmeston (1791–1867)

O brother man

When Philip Thornley, a lifelong pacifist, was allowed to go into farming instead of the armed forces, a whole new world opened up for him – one which he has never left.

When I left school in 1951, there was still conscription, and, having been brought up with Quaker views around me, I felt unable to join the army. I couldn't make this compatible with any belief in God – it seems to me the only thing we do which is the opposite of what we are trying to achieve, we deny the very thing we want to defend.

So I went before the tribunal, and I was allowed to go into alternative service. I chose farming, and it was a new world to me; it was very, very interesting, a basic, constructive job. It just seemed to suit my needs.

The views that I held then have stayed with me, and I've tried as far as I can to weave them into our life here. This pacifist view (sometimes mis-spelt and thought of as passive!) affects many things in life – trying to maintain constructive attitudes towards other people, to build relationships in a positive way, and to avoid destructive, violent types of attitudes. Really it's trying to use what Quakers call 'that of God in every man' to build our relationships. Not easy to achieve; but I think it's worthwhile.

The hymn I've chosen, 'Oh brother man, fold to thy heart thy brother', sums it up far better than I can say.

O brother man, fold to thy heart thy brother!
Where pity dwells, the peace of God is there;
To worship rightly is to love each other,
Each smile a hymn, each kindly deed a prayer.

For he whom Jesus loved hath truly spoken:
The holier worship which he deigns to bless
Restores the lost, and binds the spirit broken,
And feeds the widow and the fatherless.

Follow with reverent steps the great example
Of him whose holy work was doing good;
So shall the wide earth seem our Father's temple,
Each loving life a psalm of gratitude.

Then shall all shackles fall; the stormy clangour
Of wild war-music o'er the earth shall cease;
Love shall tread out the baleful fire of anger,
And in its ashes plant the tree of peace.

John Greenleaf Whittier (1807–92)

Philip Thornley runs a farm in the Herefordshire countryside.

Lorry driver John Downs feels that if you live in a violent area, it's easy to be violent. It's much harder to be forgiving, especially when your wife and daughter are mugged in the street.

Father, hear the prayer we offer

John Downs didn't have much time for the church until his daughter started going to the church school.

Well, Deptford's always been a tough place – you always had to look after yourself. We've always had our quota of villains and hard blokes, but they would sort of keep their trouble amongst themselves, and then it would only involve fists. But now, you'd be very cautious to interfere, with all the stabbings that go on.

I drive a lorry for a living, and when someone carves me off a slice or doesn't do what I think they should do, I don't rant and rave any more – well, no, I *do* rant and rave, but I check myself more than I used to. That's since being confirmed about five years ago. I hadn't had much to do with the church since I was a boy until our daughter, Anne, went to St James' church school, and then we got involved there. It's a very nice step to take in your life – to be confirmed as an adult.

But recently our faith was tested. One evening Marjorie, my wife, and Anne were coming home from shopping and they were mugged by three young fellas.

Marjie got knocked down, and she had to walk on a crutch for two or three weeks. Anne grappled with one of them, and she fell down and they started to kick her. They scratched all her throat and neck trying to take away a chain that she had on.

When I came home, Anne was standing there crying and the anger, you know, as a dad, that there's nothing you can do about it. I felt like rushing out and trying to find them and kill them. It's very, very difficult to be forgiving, but I think this is one of the things we must do. If we can't be forgiving, then it'll never end.

Father, hear the prayer we offer;
Not for ease that prayer shall be,
But for strength that we may ever
Live our lives courageously.

Not for ever in green pastures
Do we ask our way to be;
But the steep and rugged pathway
May we tread rejoicingly.

Not for ever by still waters
Would we idly rest and stay;
But would smite the living fountains
From the rocks along our way.

Be our strength in hours of weakness,
In our wanderings be our guide;
Through endeavour, failure, danger,
Father, be thou at our side.

Love Maria Willis (1824–1908)

The busy approaches to the Blackwall Tunnel in South-east London.

Studying to become an architect, Brian Land was found to be suffering from cancer, and given a few months to live. Here, his mother, Mary, tells how the family coped together.

Nearer, my God, to thee

Mary Land comes from Caernafon. Nearby is the magnificent scenery of Snowdonia.

How long had you to live with the knowledge that Brian had only a short time to live?

Well, the specialist told us about three months, but he actually lasted between five and six months after we brought him home.

How on earth did you cope?

Well, we were shattered of course. We were a very close knit family, and we loved each other very deeply. His two sisters were devoted to him, and he to them. And then to think that we were going to lose him . . . We got closer; we knew we had to face it and we would do it by keeping the way we were, loving him to the end.

We had his bed brought down to the lounge and we stayed with him all the time, taking turns at night. My husband kept on going to school too, to carry on with his work, which I think was the hardest part, and then coming home to inject him, to be able to carry on with the severe pain.

Do you think Brian knew?

Oh, yes, towards the end. One afternoon he asked me to prop up his legs with some pillows. I put a big bolster under his legs, because I had just realised then that he had become paralysed from the waist down. I had been warned about this – that it would happen about halfway through. And he looked at me, because he realised then what had happened.

Did it make you feel that in some way you had failed?

Oh, yes. One afternoon he dropped off to sleep and suddenly woke up and said: 'Oh, Mam, what a face! You look so miserable and everything going so well! We'll be moving to the new house soon and then you'll have your flowers.' Well, I felt ashamed, then, that I'd let him down. But I'd been thinking: 'Where have I gone wrong? I must have failed somewhere for him to get this.' And for months after his death I tortured myself, until I realised that I could put this over to God and he'd take it off me.

When she lost her son Brian, Mary Land kept feeling God's love holding her up.

Have you always had a strong faith?

Oh, yes. I was brought up in a Christian home. My mother faced a lot in her life – she lost three daughters – but I never once heard her blaming God, and I saw her

Mary Land and her husband took turns at staying with their son through the night as his illness reached its end.

being so strong. I was shaken when I lost my son, but through it all I kept on feeling nearness, some love, holding me up.

Objectively it must have seemed a tragic waste. Do you think anything positive has come out of it?
Yes, that God sees to everything and we keep on loving each other. The hymn I've chosen is 'Nearer my God to thee'. My mother found solace, and so I became nearer all the time.

Nearer, my God, to thee,
   Nearer to thee!
E'en though it be a cross
   That raiseth me,
Still all my song would be,
'Nearer, my God, to thee,
   Nearer to thee!'

Though, like the wanderer,
   The sun gone down,
Darkness be over me,
   My rest a stone;
Yet in my dreams I'd be
Nearer, my God, to thee,
   Nearer to thee.

There let my way appear
   Steps unto heaven'
All that thou send'st to me
   In mercy given,
Angels to beckon me
Nearer, my God, to thee,
   Nearer to thee.

Then, with my waking thoughts
   Bright with thy praise,
Out of my stoney griefs
   Bethel I'll raise;
So by my woes to be
Nearer, my God, to thee,
   Nearer to thee.

Sarah Flower Adams (1805–48)

Dedication

Susan Stevens suffers from cancer, but she finds the most difficult thing to cope with is not the disease, but other people's reaction to it.

Teach me, my God and King

Susan Stevens has found that having cancer means she stops worrying about the trivial things in life.

You can almost see people crossing you off their Christmas card list. They're afraid; they're saying to themselves, like I would have done before: 'This might happen to me.' It makes them shy of you and you can see it in their faces. You want to say to them that you feel just the same inside; you may have a threat hanging over you, you may not see old age, but you don't think about it all the time.

The greatest help that people can be to someone who has cancer is to just treat them like everybody else, and not to be too aware of the fact that they have this disease.

Having cancer makes a difference to your attitude to life. I think you stop worrying about trivial things like paying the mortgage and whether the car's wearing out, whether the roof's falling in, or what you are going to do when you retire. You get everything into proportion; the important things are living and other people, beauty and happiness, and that kind of thing.

I suppose having cancer could very easily have turned me against God, but it hasn't. The disease exists; some people are going to get it, some are not. I think it has strengthened my knowledge that when you need help and comfort, it's there.

I'm not a brave sort of person; I was terrified of having cancer. When I knew I might have it, I prayed that it wouldn't be cancer. I realised afterwards that what I should have prayed for was help to cope with it, help to live my life with the disease. And, somehow, I've been able to. I have not fallen apart at the seams. I seem to have acquired a sort of strength I didn't have before, which has enabled me to carry on quite happily.

The city of Wells, Somerset, from the cathedral roof.

Teach me, my God and King,
    In all things thee to see,
And what I do in anything
    To do it as for thee.

A man that looks on glass
    On it may stay his eye;
Or if he pleaseth, through it pass,
    And then the heaven espy.

All may of thee partake:
    Nothing can be so mean,
Which with this tincture, 'For thy sake,'
    Will not grow bright and clean.

A servant with this clause
    Makes drudgery divine:
Who sweeps a room, as for thy laws,
    Makes that and the action fine.

This is the famous stone
    That turneth all to gold:
For that which God doth touch and own
    Cannot for less be told.

George Herbert (1593–1633)

What could be more shattering than finding your baby son dead in his cot? This is what happened to Kay Vernon.

O Jesus, I have promised

Timothy was born on 16th March 1981 and then, five-and-a-half months later on 1st September, he died. I went into his room in the morning, about half-past-nine, and I found him dead in his cot. I knew he was dead because he was blue. It was a cot death, so nobody knows how it happened, or why. He was a very healthy contented baby, and so we had no warning of anything at all.

It was such a shock. Luckily the lady downstairs was in – Paul had gone to work by then – and she was marvellous. I was hysterical, screaming; she calmed me down and I phoned for an ambulance.

I don't remember much about the first few days, they were very much a blur. When something like that happens, you live in a state of limbo and things go on around you.

Kay Vernon lives in Kensal Rise, West London.

O Jesus, I have promised
To serve thee to the end;
Be thou for ever near me,
My Master and my Friend;
I shall not fear the battle
If thou art by my side,
Nor wander from the pathway
If thou wilt be my guide.

O let me hear thee speaking
In accents clear and still,
Above the storms of passion,
The murmurs of self-will;
O speak to reassure me,
To hasten or control;
O speak, and make me listen,
Thou Guardian of my soul.

O Jesus, thou hast promised
To all who follow thee,
That where thou art in glory
There shall thy servant be;
And, Jesus, I have promised
To serve thee to the end!
O give me grace to follow,
My Master and my Friend.

O let me see thy footmarks
And in them plant mine own;
My hope to follow duly
Is in thy strength alone:
O guide me, call me, draw me,
Uphold me to the end;
And then in heaven receive me,
My Saviour and my Friend.

J. E. Bode (1816–74)

I think the greatest help was the rest of the people at St Mark's church. They were all as shattered as we were because they loved Timothy. Three or four in particular supported me in a tremendous way. They would ring me up practically every day just to see how I was feeling, make sure I had something to do during the day, and, if I hadn't, they'd come round or invite me out somewhere. I knew they were always there at the end of a telephone if I needed them, which I did on a couple of occasions when I was feeling really depressed.

That really is the way God worked, through his church supporting me. I was angry with God for letting it happen, but my faith is in a God who knows what it's like to suffer, and he understands how I'm feeling. I won't pretend I know why it happened, but I have grown in understanding.

When I first became a Christian, I promised Jesus I would serve him to the end of my life. There are times when it's very difficult to keep that promise, and this hymn is asking for strength and help to go on.

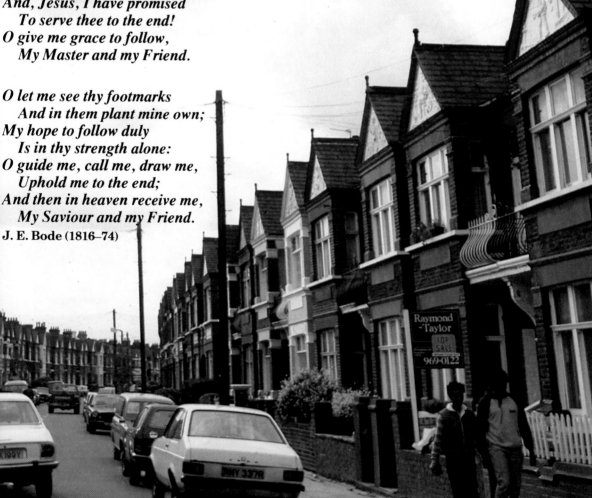

I am thine, O Lord

Eight years ago, Joan Kane was a Protestant extremist in Northern Ireland. Then something happened which made her go and apologise to all her Catholic neighbours.

Joan Kane was at one time active as a Protestant extremist in her home town of Coleraine, County Londonderry.

At that time I thought that if Ulster was going to have to fight for its rights, I would be the one to save it. I was involved in all sorts of things that I shouldn't have been – marches with hooded men, the UDA, things like that. It wasn't that I had any knowledge, even of the history of Ireland. I just wanted to be a good Protestant, and this was the only way I knew how. Through me taking leadership, the people were gullible and followed me too.

Then a series of things happened. I was very bad with rheumatoid arthritis – I couldn't lift my arm or comb my hair before midday, I used to drop things, and I even had to change the baby in the pram.

Then one day my minister came – we hadn't a very good relationship at that time – and he said that he should have been at a committee meeting, but God had told him to come and see me! He asked me if there was anything wrong with me. At the time I had a very bad

I am thine, O Lord; I have heard thy voice,
  And it told thy love to me;
But I long to rise in the arms of faith,
  And be closer drawn to thee.
    Draw me nearer, nearer, blessèd Lord,
      To the Cross where thou hast died:
    Draw me nearer, nearer, nearer, blessèd Lord,
      To thy precious, bleeding side.

    Consecrate me now to thy service, Lord,
      By the power of grace divine;
    Let my soul look up with a steadfast hope,
      And my will be lost in thine.

The Town Hall, Coleraine.

migraine but I said no. He insisted, and when I told him I had a headache, he asked if I would have any objections if he prayed for healing for me. I was very much afraid that if I allowed him to do this, God would make my pains twice as bad, but he laid his hands on me for healing and went out the door. When he lifted his hands, I had no sore head, and when he went out the front gate, I had no pains, not in my arms or my knees, no joints at all.

When you've suffered a pain for so long and all of a sudden to be released from it, you know what the power of God is. I wasn't really Christian at the time, but that started me thinking, and I started going back to church.

The first thing I was asked to do from God was to go to these Roman Catholic neighbours and apologise. For you see, in the past, I would have sat here with a machine and sewed the red, white and blue streamers and decorated all the streets. It was very conveniently arranged that the lamp-posts were in front of the Catholic homes, so we stuck the Union Jack up on those and we – I – did everything we could to abuse the situation. So I had to go and say that I was sorry, that it wouldn't happen again, and that I was trying to be a better person and serve God.

It was a very lonely time that I came through for two years, because the Protestant friends that I had didn't like me any more, they thought I was a turncoat; and the Catholic community couldn't accept me as somebody that was changed. But I knew deep within myself that it was peace that I wanted and I was finding that peace.

O the pure delight of a single hour
That before thy throne I spend,
When I kneel in prayer, and with thee, my God,
I communicate as friend with friend.

There are depths of love that I cannot know
Till I cross the narrow sea;
There are heights of joy that I may not reach
Till I rest in peace with thee.

Frances Jane van Alstyne (1820–1915)

Phyllis Burns is 'dead keen on race relations'. In the last few years she has proved it, working very hard with a group of helpers, running a class for immigrant wives to learn English and feel truly at home in Skipton.

Take my life

How did it all begin? Well, early in 1977 I heard of the need for people to teach English to immigrant wives. The headmaster of the local school was very worried because a lot of the Pakistani children were often being kept home from school to go to the shops or the doctors or the dentist to interpret for their mothers. It was decided that it would be a good idea to run a class for the mothers to learn English, so that they could do all these things for themselves.

We started with a group of about eight wives and just colour magazines to look at, because we were having to start right from nothing. We appealed for cast-off children's books, but I wasn't happy about this, because I can't bear to think I'm teaching women as if they were children.

In time we got more helpers, and grants to buy better books, and even a tape-recorder and telephones and all sorts of things to help us with our teaching. We felt that we, as helpers, ought to have some training, and eventually we won the day with a course at the local college.

At first we used to go and teach the wives in their homes, but it struck me this wasn't right. How could they be integrated into a society if they didn't come out to meet them? So we arranged for them to come out every Monday afternoon. The community centre was very kind to us, and let us go in without paying any money.

Phyllis Burns helps run regular classes where Pakistani women can learn English.

It's a struggle, because they don't attend regularly. Most of them have lots of babies, and they disappear for

Phyllis Burns comes from the town of Skipton, Yorkshire.

a while and then come back. They bring the children along, and we have toys for them to play with, and helpers to look after them, while their mothers are trying to learn.

We are trying to teach the women to understand what they see and hear, and the right expressions to use. We have lessons on going shopping, visiting the doctor, going to the clinic, how to write their names and fill in forms correctly. (This is the hardest of the lot!)

I've been to all sorts of churches and women's meetings to talk about the Pakistani women and encourage people to treat them as Skiptonians. At one time you always saw the women going shopping in twos and threes, but now I often meet them on their own in the town and they are so pleased to see everybody. It seems that they feel they belong to Skipton and are part of it.

I am a Quaker; our Pakistani women are Muslims. They are very sincere and I respect them for it. They know I'm a Christian, and accept what I do. The hymn I've chosen is: 'Take my life and let it be consecrated Lord to thee.' We all have abilities to do something in some small way to serve the community. George Fox tells us to walk cheerfully through the world, and this is what we try to do.

Take my life, and let it be
Consecrated, Lord, to thee;
Take my moments and my days,
Let them flow in ceaseless praise.

Take my hands, and let them move
At the impulse of thy love.
Take my feet, and let them be
Swift and beautiful for thee.

Take my voice, and let me sing
Always, only, for my King;
Take my lips, and let them be
Filled with messages from thee.

Take my silver and my gold;
Not a mite would I withhold.
Take my intellect, and use
Every power as thou shalt choose.

Take my will, and make it thine:
It shall be no longer mine.
Take my heart: it is thine own;
It shall be thy royal throne.

Take my love; my Lord, I pour
At thy feet its treasure-store.
Take myself, and I will be
Ever, only, all for thee.
Frances R. Havergal (1836–79)

Going blind in his teens did not seem to Keith Russell like a loss. 'No, I have gained,' he says. 'My eyes have been opened towards life.'

Be thou my Vision

Although I was born blind, partial sight returned when I was about eighteen months old and I led an ordinary life, going to a sighted school. Throughout my school life I had difficulty with reading books and the blackboard, but with the help and patience of many teachers I was able to continue my studies until the age of sixteen.

At this stage my sight had begun to deteriorate through a condition called glaucoma, and the local authority put me in touch with The Royal National College for the Blind at Hereford. I came for assessment and was accepted. It took off from there!

Since coming to Hereford, I have gained greater confidence in myself and made many new friends. I am a

Keith Russell has a trained guide-dog, a yellow labrador named Farley.

member of the church youth group and also enjoy drama, athletics and working with handicapped children during college holidays.

I am doing a four-year business studies course which consists of audio-typing and 'O' level studies. An essential part of the course is the home economics and living skills, because you can be a highly-trained typist or piano-tuner but still need to be able to fend for yourself. I have also received training with a guide-dog, a yellow labrador called Farley.

I eventually want to go on and do welfare work with handicapped children because I'm always being helped, and it's a relief to know you can help someone else.

The Royal National College for the Blind at Hereford.

A lot of people look upon blindness as being cut off from the world. This is not true. Blindness may cut you off from things, but not from people. Things are immaterial – people aren't.

I've chosen the hymn 'Be thou my Vision'. The words are very apt because I look upon my faith now as being my vision.

Be thou my Vision, O Lord of my heart,
Be all else but naught to me, save that thou art;
Be thou my best thought in the day and the night,
Both waking and sleeping, thy presence my light.

Be thou my Wisdom, be thou my true Word;
Be thou ever with me, and I with thee, Lord;
Be thou my great Father, and I thy true son;
Be thou in me dwelling, and I with thee one.

Be thou my breastplate, my sword for the fight;
Be thou my whole armour, be thou my true might;
Be thou my soul's shelter, be thou my strong tower,
O raise thou me heavenward, great Power of my power.

Riches I heed not, nor man's empty praise,
Be thou mine inheritance now and always;
Be thou and thou only the first in my heart;
O Sovereign of heaven, my treasure thou art.

High King of heaven, thou heaven's bright Sun,
O grant me its joys, after victory is won;
Great Heart of my own heart, whatever befall,
Still be thou my Vision, O Ruler of all.

Ancient Irish. Tr. Mary Elizabeth Byrne (1881–1931)
Versified by Eleanor Henrietta Hull (1861–1935)

The Revd Dr Kenneth Greet is Secretary of the Methodist Conference.

Thou God of truth and love

I think that hymns are immensely important. As John Wesley put it in his rather quaint way in the preface to the Methodist hymnbook, here you have a compendium of theology. Any churchman who stands up and takes the hymnbook in his hand is holding a comprehensive summary of the deep theological beliefs of his church. And whether we want to be or not – and these days most of us want to be – you've got to be an ecumenist if you sing hymns.

Take the Methodist hymnbook, as we call it; you will find hymns by Anglicans, Baptists, Roman Catholics, the lot. So the hymnbook is one of the most ecumenical documents you can think of.

I think hymns are a unique way of enabling people to express their highest and deepest feelings about God and about the faith which makes Christians tick. Often the marrying of appropriate words to appropriate music triggers off something – I can't define it more clearly than that – inside the believer. I think this is the experience of all of us who sing hymns.

The City Road Chapel, London, has long been an important centre for Methodism. Wesley's house stands beside it.

This statue of John Wesley, the indefatigable preacher, stands outside London's City Road Chapel.

The Revd Dr Kenneth Greet.

And also there's this fact, never to be forgotten, which I think *Songs of Praise* brings out again and again, that a particular hymn that may not mean overmuch to you or me means an immense amount to the person who's chosen it as his favourite hymn because of some circumstance with which that hymn is associated. And so a moment of great importance – of joy or of sorrow – is forever linked with the sound of that music and the sound of those words.

Thou God of truth and love,
  We seek thy perfect way,
Ready thy choice to approve,
  thy providence to obey:
Enter into thy wise design,
And sweetly lose our will in thine.

Why hast thou cast our lot
  In the same age and place,
And why together brought
  To see each other's face;
To join with loving sympathy,
And mix our friendly souls in thee?

Didst thou not make us one,
  That we might one remain,
Together travel on,
  And bear each other's pain;
Till all thy utmost goodness prove,
And rise renewed in perfect love?

Then let us ever bear
  The blessèd end in view,
And join, with mutual care,
  To fight our passage through;
And kindly help each other on,
Till all receive the starry crown.

O may thy Spirit seal
  Our souls unto that day,
With all thy fullness fill,
  And then transport away:
Away to our eternal rest,
Away to our Redeemer's breast.

Charles Wesley (1707–88)

When Maisie Hill plucked up courage to go into her local church, a lot of things in her life changed.

How sweet the name of Jesus sounds

Maisie Hill lives in Battersea, South London.

I had a lot of worry and depression and I couldn't take no more. I passed this church several times and wondered whether to walk into it. When I did, I found that I was welcome, nobody turned their back on me, and I've been coming ever since. The vicar has taught me everything I know, and the parish worker has been there when I needed her. (And, believe me, there've been times when I have!) I know I can always turn to them, and I can turn to God, because God has given me all the strength I need.

I used to row a lot with people, but then, if you go to church, you don't row. Alright, there is people that still row, but then you have to take it with a pinch of salt. I just hope that I can draw more people into our church and get the love that I've had.

I come every Sunday if possible. Sometimes I don't come at evenings because I have my grand-daughter living with me (and I must admit she plays up of a morning). I walk in the door and I pick up my books from the table. I touch the radiator to see if it's on first, and then I sit there and get this lovely feeling. It's like you are not crushed together, but it's like somebody saying, well, you're settled there to listen so watch and listen.

People have been so sweet to me. It's a wonderful world, and God has given me everything I have. I'm not posh or anything, but everybody loves me, and I send out my love to everybody.

Maisie Hill found a welcome in her local church when she most needed it.

How sweet the name of Jesus sounds
  In a believer's ear!
It soothes his sorrows, heals his wounds,
  And drives away his fear.

It makes the wounded spirit whole,
  And calms the troubled breast;
'Tis manna to the hungry soul,
  And to the weary rest.

Dear name! the rock on which I build,
  My shield and hiding-place,
My never-failing treasury filled
  With boundless stores of grace.

Jesus! my Shepherd, Brother, Friend,
  My Prophet, Priest, and King,
My Lord, my Life, my Way, my End,
  Accept the praise I bring.

Weak is the effort of my heart,
  And cold my warmest thought;
But when I see thee as thou art,
  I'll praise thee as I ought.

Till then I would thy love proclaim
  With every fleeting breath;
And may the music of thy name
  Refresh my soul in death.

John Newton (1725–1807)

Steve Robinson has very poor hearing. His wife, Carol, is totally deaf. But, with their faith and determination, they cope with the frustrations and hurt that this can bring.

Just as I am

I've always had a handicap – I was born with it – but it really started to become a problem just after I left school. I used to mix with people, go out to parties, that sort of thing, and find that I was missing things. Because of all the hubbub, the background noise, I couldn't quite understand what people were saying. I would keep going Sorry? Pardon? Can you say that again, or, worse, misunderstanding what people had said.

Sometimes people were quite unkind, shouting things like: 'Turn your deaf-aid up!' And sometimes you start thinking people are talking about you – you can get quite paranoid! But you have to develop a thick skin and learn to laugh with people, rather than get resentful about them laughing at you.

One of the biggest problems was getting a job. Prospective employers are wary of taking on people with hearing handicaps because of things like using the telephone. I really wanted to join the armed forces, but I didn't get past the recruiting officer's door because of

Although Steve Robinson has a hearing handicap, he holds down a full-time job.

Just as I am, without one plea
But that thy blood was shed for me,
And that thou bidst me come to thee,
    O Lamb of God, I come.

Just as I am, and waiting not
To rid my soul of one dark blot,
To thee, whose blood can cleanse
    each spot,
    O Lamb of God, I come.

Just as I am – though tossed about
With many a conflict, many a doubt,
Fightings and fears within, without,
    O Lamb of God, I come.

Just as I am – poor, wretched, blind –
Sight, riches, healing of the mind,
Yea, all I need, in thee to find,
    O Lamb of God, I come.

Just as I am, thou wilt receive,
Wilt welcome, pardon, cleanse, relieve;
Because thy promise I believe,
    O Lamb of God, I come.

Just as I am – thy love unknown
Has broken every barrier down;
Now to be thine, yea, thine alone,
    O Lamb of God, I come.

Just as I am, of that free love
The breadth, length, depth and
    height to prove,
Here for a season, then above,
    O Lamb of God, I come.

Charlotte Elliott (1789–1871)

the hearing handicap. But now I'm employed as a media resources officer in the education field, making, rather ironically, audio-visual aids for the classroom!

My wife, Carol, is totally deaf, and I am her link with the hearing world. In a conversation with anyone else, I have to turn to her and sign to her what's being said. And we have had to make adaptations to the house like a flashing light for the doorbell and the telephone, so that she can carry on as normally as possible.

I have to be very careful because it is so frustrating – you get this feeling, you can hear the hubbub of voices and things and you're looking at peoples' faces trying to read their lips and, if you can't fully understand what they're saying, you have to keep your temper in check and not let it rip. This is one of the ways in which my faith has helped me. When I get these feelings of rage and want to go out and smash everything up or kick the cat, I sort of think to myself: 'No, that's not the way to behave. Think carefully, pray about it and come rationally back to yourself.'

I've chosen the hymn, 'Just as I am', because I like to say: 'Well, Lord this is how I am, I'm not a perfect specimen by any means, but I'm prepared to work for you.'

Steve Robinson works near County Hall in central London.

Is it possible that a baby born with severe heart and lung defects could be cured by prayer and without surgery? This is what happened to Patricia Redfern's baby son, Adam.

Blessed assurance

The Redfern family come from Skipton, Yorkshire.

Adam was born with club feet – they told me just as he was born. And after a few weeks they found out that he also had a heart murmur. He was a very sick baby, and they transferred him to Brompton Heart Hospital in London, and it was there that they explained to me exactly what was wrong. He had an enlarged heart, with a small hole in it, causing the murmur; in addition an artery was blocked and one of his lungs deflated.

It was then they decided that they wanted to do this special test on him – on the Thursday afternoon – and I had to sign the consent form because of the risk. Meanwhile all the churches around were praying for him to be healed, to come through it; but I had a deep assurance in my heart that all was going to be well.

On Thursday evening I phoned the hospital and spoke to the sister. I said: 'How is Adam? How did the test go?' And she said: 'There's nothing wrong with him.' I thought she meant there was no hole in the heart, but she said: 'There's nothing there at all; everything's perfectly all-right, normal.'

I went in to see him the next day, and the doctors were round his bed, absolutely amazed. They said: 'Isn't it marvellous, Mrs Redfern. You've got a perfect baby, you just need to have those feet right now.' It was marvellous. I'd heard of people being healed before, but when it happens to you it really shakes you.

Some of the people who had been praying for him accepted it, but some of them couldn't believe it. I felt hurt, I don't know why, that they had been praying for him, yet they couldn't accept that their prayers were answered.

The hymn I have chosen is 'Blessed assurance, Jesus is mine'. I had this deep assurance when Adam was so ill.

Patricia Redfern with her young son, Adam.

Blessed assurance, Jesus is mine:
O what a foretaste of glory divine!
Heir of salvation, purchase of God;
Born of his Spirit, washed in his blood.

Chorus:
This is my story, this is my song,
Praising my Saviour all the day long.

Perfect submission, perfect delight,
Visions of rapture burst on my sight;
Angels descending, bring from above
Echoes of mercy, whispers of love.

Perfect submission, all is at rest
I in my Saviour am happy and blest;
Watching and waiting, looking above,
Filled with his goodness, lost in his love.
Frances Jane van Alstyne (1820–1915)

May the mind of Christ my Saviour

It was an almost idyllic childhood for Trudi Greengrass and her brother and sister until the war came, and with it the Russian advance into Lower Silesia, where they lived.

Living in East Germany, in the winter we had a very cold climate. My father had horses, and he would take us for rides in the forest in his sled, bells jingling round the horses' necks. This is the kind of childhood I look back on because, although it was war-time, we didn't have any bombing and so on, we never knew anything about war.

Then one day it all changed. It was in February, and my father talked of leaving home because the Russians were advancing. We got things ready, but we never got away because the Russians came in early next morning. It was scaring; there were planes coming and bombs. My father took us and we fled into the forest. By lunch-time we went back to our house and it was terrible – the Russians had literally thrown everything out of the house. You had to climb over everything; food was mixed with clothes.

A lot of Russians came, and asked for my father's name. Because it was a bit unusual that he was not a soldier, I think they thought he was a great Nazi, you know, and that's when this very sad thing happened. The Russians took my mother and my father and us children into their bedroom. They raped my mother in front of my father, and then they took him. I shall never forget him walking along the garden path. He had his riding gear on, and he just looked back and waved. That was the last time we ever saw him.

And then life went on. It was absolutely scaring. It went on like this until the end of the war in May, and in all that time we never undressed; we just huddled together in rooms. Russians would come in, take women, children, anybody really. Some never came back. We didn't have anything – water, electricity, not even soap. We lived on anything we could find; it's amazing what you can think of doing when the need arises. There were plenty of potatoes. Germans always had a lot of potatoes, and we made starch from them. We gathered up sugar from the ruins of a nearby sugar factory, and we found ways of purifying salt from the

The last time Trudi Greengrass saw her father, he was being led away by Russian soldiers.

salt-tulic blocks in the neighbouring farms. But as time went on, we were actually hungry and we looked terrible – dirty and neglected, and we had lice and fleas and terrible boils.

Eventually we were gathered up one night in the market-square, and, after walking for miles, we were loaded into cattle trucks and told we were going to be sent to a refugee camp.

Then, when we eventually arrived in West Germany, a wonderful thing happened. We met a young man who, though he had gone through the same sort of experience, seemed terribly relaxed and happy. He invited us to the Baptist church in the next town and, as we walked in, we experienced a most wonderful love from people around us. We looked pretty sad and poverty stricken, and they showed such concern. The third night that we went to this church, the preacher was talking about how wonderful Christ's love is. It didn't mean a lot to me – I still had this dreadful fear within – but at this moment I felt a wonderful peace come over me as if Christ's arms were round me. And this peace has never left me.

I have chosen the hymn, 'May the mind of Christ my Saviour live in me from day to day'. It is a prayer, and I would like to think that it is mine.

May the mind of Christ my Saviour
  Live in me from day to day,
By his love and power controlling
  All I do and say.

May the Word of God dwell richly
  In my heart from hour to hour,
So that all may see I triumph
  Only through his power.

May the peace of God my Father
  Rule my life in everything,
That I may be calm to comfort
  Sick and sorrowing.

May the love of Jesus fill me,
  As the waters fill the sea;
Him exalting, self abasing,
  This is victory.

May I run the race before me,
  Strong and brave to face the foe,
Looking only unto Jesus
  As I onward go.

May his beauty rest upon me
  As I seek the lost to win,
And may they forget the channel,
  Seeing only him.

Kate Barclay Wilkinson

Blest are the pure in heart

From routine calls to emergency dashes, ambulance driver Gerald Lush finds that his faith helps him face whatever his daily work brings.

Well, we cover the whole spectrum of ambulance work, from emergencies, urgent cases to be taken into hospital by doctor's orders, to the social and clinic work. Some of these are patients that can walk out and be taken in a one-man sitting case vehicle, or sometimes two men have to lift them into an ambulance, or even take them in their own wheelchair.

We have a very special relationship with some of the regulars in their wheelchairs – always a laugh and a joke with them. Some can't speak very well: we have to sit and listen and try to understand them, and share in

Taunton, Somerset.

their little jokes they try to tell us. Very often with some of these disabled we take them home, turn on their gas fire for them, even change a light bulb maybe. It's that sort of thing I like doing – the social side. And we have a grand time with them at Christmas, the geriatric ones; we take them home, singing carols all the way round the town, delivering them home. They enjoy that, and we do as well.

My faith helps me a lot. When I started on the service there were times when, going to a road accident, I would feel inadequate. I didn't know if I was doing enough. Sometimes I would panic. But since committing myself to Christ I find no need to panic. I can go on steadily and do the job with calmness, which helps the patients as well. If they see there is someone firmly in control of the situation, that helps them and stops the shock.

A few years ago, there was a train – the night sleeper – that caught fire about 3 o'clock in the morning. I was called out to it and we worked for twelve hours solid, and I think if it wasn't for my faith, I'd have been much more disturbed by the whole thing. Knowing that when there is a death, no matter how, whether it's dramatic or if it's a natural death, there is an end, a good end, not a sudden shut-off, my faith helps me understand it in a way.

Blest are the pure in heart,
For they shall see our God;
The secret of the Lord is theirs,
Their soul is Christ's abode.

The Lord, who left the heavens
Our life and peace to bring,
To dwell in lowliness with men,
Their pattern and their King;

Still to the lowly soul
He doth himself impart,
And for his dwelling and his throne
Chooseth the pure in heart.

Lord, we thy presence seek;
May ours this blessing be;
Give us a pure and lowly heart,
A temple meet for thee.

JOHN KEBLE (1792-1866)

Hymns for Special Occasions

Eternal Father

With most of his family mariners or fishermen, it was inevitable that Ernie McMieken should go to sea. But in the 1920s it was not easy to find a job.

Both my mother and father were born in the Isle of Man, and all the family were fishermen – master-mariners or trawler-masters. They all had fishing roots, so I had to follow the sea too. I went to the fishing with my father but after four years I got rather disgruntled, packed a sea-bag and went off to Liverpool to try my luck.

Peel harbour, Isle of Man.

The Liverpool docks were pretty quiet at that time, but I was fortunate enough to sign on an old tramp

Eternal Father, strong to save,
Whose arm doth bind the restless wave,
Who bidd'st the mighty ocean deep
Its own appointed limits keep:
  O hear us when we cry to thee
  For those in peril on the sea!

O Saviour, whose almighty word
The winds and waves submissive heard,
Who walkedst on the foaming deep,
And calm amid its rage didst sleep:
  O hear us when we cry to thee
  For those in peril on the sea!

O Holy Spirit, who didst brood
Upon the chaos dark and rude,
Who bad'st its angry tumult cease,
And gavest light, and life, and peace:
  O hear us when we cry to thee
  For those in peril on the sea!

O Trinity of love and power,
Our brethren shield in danger's hour;
From rock and tempest, fire and foe,
Protect them wheresoe'er they go;
  And ever let there rise to thee
  Glad hymns of praise from land and sea.
William Whiting (1825–78)

steamer. After a short trip of a couple of months we arrived back in Liverpool to lay up; no trade, so you had to look for another ship. That's the way it went.

Then about 1928 I signed up with the Isle of Man Company, with whom I stayed until 1972, and began studying for my various tickets. To become a ship's master in the local service you had to study for a Mersey pilot's licence, Belfast pilot's licence, Morecambe Bay pilot's licence, and an Ardrossan pilot's licence.

Although I'm retired now, after fifty years at sea, I still have links with the sea and sailors. Quite a number of masters and engineers retired about the time I did, and we formed ourselves into a little musical group called 'The Mariners'. We sing in various churches on the Isle of Man. When we take a service we always start with the sea-farers' hymn – 'Eternal Father, strong to save.' So naturally that is the hymn I have chosen.

Ernie McMieken was a master mariner before he retired from the sea.

A farmworker with the harvests of thirty years behind him, Peter Hambrook feels he comes close to God in his life on the farm.

The Parish Church, Great Mongeham, Kent.

Fair waved the golden corn

It's the job I chose when I left school, and unfortunately I've been doing it ever since – or fortunately! I left school on a Friday and started here on the Saturday morning, and the Guvnor says to me, 'If you're any good after six weeks, I'll keep you on'! My first job on the farm was filling up petrol cans for the combine harvester. These days I'm a general sort of odd-job – if anything's broken, I repair it.

But at harvest-time, I'm a combine operator. I think it's a great honour to drive a combine, a sought-after job on the farm. You get this great feeling of power, sitting

Fair waved the golden corn
In Canaan's pleasant land,
When full of joy, some shining morn,
Went forth the reaper-band.

To God so good and great
Their cheerful thanks they pour;
Then carry to his temple-gate
The choicest of their store.

Peter Hambrook says he is a 'general sort of odd-job' on the farm.

up there in this enormous machine. It has a personality about it, a combine. You go along there and you say: 'Come on old girl, don't clap out on me tonight, love. I'll try and find the rattle in the morning.' I suppose you're praying about it all the while as you go along.

It's a fantastic feeling, the harvest. The whole year's work is coming to a climax. You put your seed in, wheat or barley, it germinates, you've watched it grow. It's a miracle, the miracle of life. I can see beauty in farming, in agriculture, in fields of corn.

But the day after harvest is horrible. Nobody speaks to each other. You could nearly sit down and cry. I get the job of washing the machines down and putting them away. Summer's over, there's people burning off their stubbles, the evenings are drawing in, damp dewy mornings. The birds start heading for home.

But then you know that Christmas is coming, and after that, you're away again. You live the whole cycle of the year. It's superb.

There is always new work to be done on the farm.

For thus the holy word
Spoken by Moses ran:
'The first-ripe ears are for the Lord,
The rest he gives to man.'

Great Mongeham, Kent.

Like Israel, Lord, we give
Our earliest fruits to thee,
And pray that, long as we shall live,
We may thy servants be.

John Hampden Gurney (1802–62)
Based on Exodus 22, 29

We plough the fields and scatter

Philip Davies finds there is a kind of mystery about driving his lorry through the night.

We deliver cider and pectin all over the country, as far north as Glasgow, and as far south as Cornwall. We get addicted to the job because, although we work awkward shifts and work when other people possibly wouldn't enjoy working at all, being as we're high up in the cab of a lorry, driving around at night or in the early hours of the morning, there's a kind of mystery about the job that makes it all the more enthralling.

I see how other people live, how other people travel, how other people get on with their lives.

We see the changing seasons from winter through to spring, spring through to summer, summer through to autumn, and the distinct changes of things. The farmers

We plough the fields, and scatter
The good seed on the land,
But it is fed and watered
By God's Almighty hand:
He sends the snow in winter,
The warmth to swell the grain,
The breezes, and the sunshine,
And soft, refreshing rain.
All good gifts around us
Are sent from heaven above;
Then thank the Lord, O thank the Lord,
For all his love.

are always busy in the fields, either planting seeds or reaping corn and hay. This leads me to believe that there is a far greater force than some people would like to believe, making these things happen.

Similarly, the birth and growth of my three children have also been an extremely strong influence over my beliefs. Seeing children born is, well, if you've never seen it, then you've missed something colossal. Words can hardly cover it. But it does lead you to believing in this super-power that a lot of people can't find their way clear to believe in.

But it can be sort of hard, believing in God, when you travel around like I do, when you come up against all sorts of accidents. People sometimes get killed; you just have to say – God moves in a mysterious way.

As I'm driving along I think of the hymns that I sing in church every Sunday, particularly the one I've chosen – 'We plough the fields and scatter' – it's one of my favourites.

Philip Davies is a truck driver for a larger cider-making firm in Herefordshire. What some would call a boring job with unsocial hours, he finds satisfying and thought-provoking.

Philip Davies lives near the beautiful cathedral city of Hereford.

He only is the Maker
 Of all things near and far;
He paints the wayside flower,
 He lights the evening star;
The winds and waves obey him,
 By him the birds are fed;
Much more to us, his children,
 He gives our daily bread.
  All good gifts around us
  Are sent from heaven above;
  Then thank the Lord, O thank the Lord,
  For all his love.

We thank thee then, O Father,
 For all things bright and good,
The seed-time and the harvest,
 Our life, our health, our food.
Accept the gifts we offer
 For all thy love imparts,
And, what thou most desirest,
 Our humble, thankful hearts.
  All good gifts around us
  Are sent from heaven above;
  Then thank the Lord, O thank the Lord,
  For all his love.

M. Claudius (1740–1815)
Tr. Jane M. Campbell (1817–78)

Ronald Dove has been a bell-ringer for over sixty years. He has rung the bells of nearly four and a half thousand churches.

For all the saints

When did you first become interested in bell-ringing?
When I was at school, but I didn't have the opportunity until I joined the church. I was nineteen at the time. It wasn't easy to get into the belfry in those days; I had to ask about three times, and wait several months, but I managed to persuade somebody to teach me to ring, and once I got into the belfry I really settled in.

Is there a fellowship among bell-ringers?
There's a saying that if a ringer in a strange town hears bells and makes his way to the belfry, he is immediately among friends. I can vouch for the veracity of that.

Why do you think it's important that a church should have bells?
Nowadays the only purpose, as far as the church is concerned, is for the bells to act as a witness. In the olden days, of course, when people were restricted to their parishes and didn't have watches, the bell served a genuine purpose as a call bell.

Is your bell-ringing simply an interesting hobby or is it more than that?
I regard my ringing on a Sunday as an act of worship, an act of witness.

York Minster.

For all the saints who from their labours rest,
Who thee by faith before the world confessed,
Thy name, O Jesu, be for ever blest.
                    Alleluia.

Thou wast their rock, their fortress, and their might;
Thou, Lord, their Captain in the well-fought fight;
Thou, in the darkness, still their one true Light.
                    Alleluia.

O may thy soldiers, faithful, true, and bold,
Fight as the saints who nobly fought of old,
And win, with them, the victor's crown of gold.
                    Alleluia.

O blest communion, fellowship divine!
We feebly struggle, they in glory shine;
Yet all are one in thee, for all are thine.
                    Alleluia.

And when the strife is fierce, the warfare long,
Steals on the ear the distant triumph-song,
And hearts are brave again and arms are strong.
                    Alleluia.

The golden evening brightens in the west;
Soon, soon to faithful warriors comes their rest:
Sweet is the calm of Paradise the blest.
                    Alleluia.

But lo, there breaks a yet more glorious day;
The saints triumphant rise in bright array:
The King of Glory passes on his way.
                    Alleluia.

From earth's wide bounds, from ocean's farthest coast,
Through gates of pearl streams in the countless host,
Singing to Father, Son, and Holy Ghost
                    Alleluia.

W. Walsham How (1823–97)

Ronald Dove finds there is a fellowship among bell-ringers.

Four years a soldier, Geoff Stanley finds that his very private religion helps sustain him in the rigours of army life.

Jerusalem

I've been in the army now just four years. I decided to join because there was no job satisfaction in civvie street. Plus, round our way, it was very hard to find a job, though I did find one or two. So I went to the Careers Office and, three weeks later, I signed on for nine years.

I'm enjoying it. Everybody takes the army for doing things like learning how to fire a rifle, but we do other things as well like skiing, skating and all sorts of sports activities. Plus other trades; you get drivers and radio operators, which can come in useful after you've left the army.

I've been interested in religion since I was eight or nine, and it's just built up from there, with changes now and then to different views and feelings. I've just carried on my own religion to myself.

I believe you should be able to pray wherever you are. I mean, you could be sat in the middle of a training area in a tank for instance. You learn to accommodate yourself to pray in whatever place you are. It's a comfort – a help – to find a way that you can relieve yourself if you have done anything wrong. And a relaxation from the strain of the job; it might sound easy to sit in a tank trundling round the countryside looking through a sight with a big gun swinging around, but you really do strain the senses and the mind. Or after the morning battle PT, when you literally crawl away from the gym. You just sit there and gain comfort from praying.

Some people will scoff at you for it, or they joke – 'He's probably going into his room for a quick prayer.' Or – 'Is he going to get his prayer mat out again?' But it's nothing offensive, they don't try to hurt you or make you angry. I just pass it by. It doesn't bother me at all.

I have chosen the song 'Jerusalem' because it expresses a feeling of pride in the country of England and of building one's life on a foundation.

Sometimes people mock Geoff Stanley for his religion. It doesn't bother him.

And did those feet in ancient time
*   Walk upon England's mountains green?*
And was the holy Lamb of God
*   On England's pleasant pastures seen?*
And did the countenance divine
*   Shine forth upon our clouded hills?*
And was Jerusalem builded here
*   Among those dark satanic mills?*

Bring me my bow of burning gold!
*   Bring me my arrows of desire!*
Bring me my spear! O clouds, unfold!
*   Bring me my chariot of fire!*
I will not cease from mental fight,
*   Nor shall my sword sleep in my hand,*
Till we have built Jerusalem
*   In England's green and pleasant land.*

William Blake (1757–1827)